Contents

iv / *The Many Arts of Sales Management*

21022929 9

This book to be returned on or before
the date stamped below.

THE
MANY
ARTS
OF
SALES
MANAGEMENT

MICHAEL BEER

McGRAW-HILL Book Company (UK) Limited

London · New York · St Louis · San Francisco · Auckland · Bogotá
Guatemala · Hamburg · Johannesburg · Lisbon · Madrid · Mexico
Montreal · New Delhi · Panama · Paris · San Juan · São Paulo
Singapore · Sydney · Tokyo · Toronto

First published in Radnor, Pennsylvania, by Chilton Book Company and simultaneously in Don Mills, Ontario, Canada, by Thomas Nelson & Sons Ltd.

This edition published by
McGRAW-HILL Book Company (UK) Limited
MAIDENHEAD · BERKSHIRE · ENGLAND

British Library Cataloguing in Publication Data

Beer, Michael
    The many arts of sales management.
    1. Sales management
    I. Title
    658.8'1   HF5438.4
    ISBN 0-07-084562-X

Library of Congress Cataloging in Publication Data

Beer, Michael, 1926-
    The many arts of sales management.

    Includes index.
    1. Sales management.   I. Title.
    HF5438.4.B43   1981   658.8'1   81-6011
    ISBN 0-07-084562-X   AACR2

12345M.B.84321

Printed and bound in Great Britain by Mansell Bookbinders Ltd.

Foreword

The true role and importance of selling and its contribution to the economy, industry and commerce is at last gaining a long overdue recognition.

Selling is one of the few remaining disciplines where through personal endeavour, enterprise and effort, an individual can render a positive contribution to his or her company and in so doing enjoy a measure of job satisfaction.

It follows that in order to ensure efficient, successful and profitable sales, not only must the sales management be experienced in all facets of selling, but also respected for its demonstrable capability in the face of the problems and opportunities that will be encountered.

Michael Beer's grasp and depth of understanding of the multi-interfacing, interacting disciplines of sales management is excellent. His style of writing, the detail provided, not only renders the book informative and interesting, but rather a *must* for all who wish or need to have at their disposal, a first class exposition of the Arts of Sales Management.

Michael Beer's work is unhesitantly recommended to all existing and aspiring practitioners of sales management.

Keith Brauer
Director-General
The Institute of Sales Management

Why This Book?

You don't really care why I decided to write this book. But let me tell you nevertheless that my reason is simply that after waiting for half my business life for someone else to write it, it finally dawned on me that no one would. Not, heaven knows, that there is any shortage of reading matter on management. In fact, if any working manager were to attempt to read even a fraction of the books and magazines on management which pour off the presses, he would rapidly cease to be a working manager at all; he would become a theoretician, and no amount of theorizing by itself ever made a profit.

This book is intended to be completely practical. Any odd bits of theory are included only as a framework on which to build procedures that work. It is a sort of manual for the person who is in charge of a group of salesmen.* Titles seldom mean very much in business, and this person may be called sales manager, district manager, area supervisor, field trainer, branch manager, or even (erroneously) marketing manager. The title is not important, the job is. He is the person responsible for hiring, training, motivating, controlling, organizing, and running a sales team. If you are such a person then every word in the book was written with you in mind. If you are not this person, then read no further—there is nothing here for you.

*See "A Word on Women in Sales," page 2.

1

MANAGING A TEAM

What follows will not make your job easy; nothing in the world will do that. You are paid to run a successful, profitable, and company-oriented group, and this group of yours consists not of dutiful clerks or subservient laborers, but of free-thinking, outgoing, independent, and potentially rebellious salesmen, and they are more difficult to manage than any other people in business. Proof of this: a man who works in the accounting department of an office is usually easier to manage as he become better at his job, but the very reverse is usually the case with salesmen. No sales manager has to be told that as a salesman becomes better at selling, he often becomes harder to manage; he knows how good he is and he tends to resent what he considers to be petty rules and restrictions which should apply only to the run-of-the-mill salesrep and not to the star. The average salesman is much easier to manage, but you can't win with him. It is the star who gives you the sales figures, and it is the star who can be a pain in the neck to handle.

No, managing a sales team will never be an easy job. As I have tried to emphasize in the chapter headings, it is an art. And because it is an art there can be very few rigid rules—a few basic axioms, perhaps, but long lists of rules won't help you, and you won't find them here. There are points which I believe are worthy of consideration and these I have included and discussed, but you will modify them, expand them, adapt them, or reject them entirely, depending on your particular management situation and your own personal management philosophy. And speaking of your particular situation, a small digression is, if not mandatory, certainly in order.

A WORD ON WOMEN IN SALES

In this book I constantly refer to "salesmen," and when I need a name or a pronoun I use male names and talk about "him," I assert, however, that I am no male chauvinist pig, and unlike many men who disclaim MCP tendencies and yet still act as though they are the master sex, I really am not. My work brings me in touch with far too many successful women to have any illusions about man's superiority in business. I regularly run sales and management clinics with a mixture of men and women, and some with women only, and any man who is still clinging grimly to the crumbling bastions of male supremacy would be shaken to the core if he sat in on some of these.

I have found women who are completely lost in the selling business, who should never have entered it in the first place, but of course this applies equally to men. I have also had women in sales and management clinics who were so far ahead of the men that they made them look like bumbling novices.

No, my reason for talking about "salesmen" is simply one of convenience. I dislike the clumsiness of "salesperson," and the cause of male chauvinism has made the word "saleswoman" faintly derogatory—as bad as "authoress" for a woman writer.

There is one question, though, which regularly comes up in my management clinics: "Do women make competent salespeople, and what differences are there in managing them compared with men?" Two questions, really. To look at the second part first, my initial reaction is: why should there be any difference? Women are people before they are women, and people problems are people problems. This is true as far as it goes, but it begs the question, because in addition to being people, women are also women, and they *are* different from men; not better or worse—different.

It might be as well to ask: why women in selling at all? Is there any type of selling at which they would be better than men, simply because they are women? I did once think so, but I have changed my mind on this. Apart from over-the-counter retail selling of such obvious products as cosmetics and clothing, where the woman customer would probably feel more rapport with another woman, there seems to be little to choose between men and women. Oddly enough, most perfumes and cosmetics, for instance, are sold to chain stores and supermarkets by men.

There is a feeling that an attractive woman will find it easier to sell to a male than a man would. Most women in selling will deny this vigorously, and I believe they are right. As one very attractive (and successful) woman said to me; "He might find me a more pleasant sight in his office than the average man, but when it comes to signing an order he is interested in only one thing, and it isn't my cleavage. It's whether or not he is getting the best product for the job." Right. The cleavage might just get the interview, but it won't get the order, and in any case, that isn't the way the best women in selling do the job.

Are there, then, any types of selling for which women are obviously unsuitable? Not as silly a question as it sounds, although such fields as heavy industrial equipment spring to the mind. As soon as someone mentions a product which seems banned to women, some manager will tell of a woman selling building supplies, diesel locomotives, or front-end loaders, and doing a terrific job. Women have already invaded the motor industry and the real estate business, and they seem determined to branch out into every type of selling there is. Resistance is disappearing, too. As one manager said to me, "I hire my people on one criterion only—whether they can do the job. And I don't give a damn whether they shave under their arms or under their noses."

Well and good, and now let us try to answer the part of the question we have so far been dodging.

The difference between running men and women in a sales team is not in technique or direction, it is simply in degree. I am talking broadly here, but women in selling respond in the same way as men to counseling, instruction, and discipline—they simply respond *more*. They will react more positively to good human relations, to thoughtfulness, to pleasant working conditions, and to recognition of effort. They will react more negatively to unfairness, to harsh reprimanding, to not being taken seriously, and to neglect in the field.

It is a cliche to say that women are more emotional than men. I think the truth is that they merely show their emotions more readily than men, and this to me makes women easier to manage, not harder. If one of your salesmen is bugged by something and bottles it up inside himself, you have little chance of defining the problem and helping him. At least a woman's emotions are usually right there on display and she will be more willing to discuss her problem with you.

Which brings us to the reason that so many male managers fear having women on their sales teams. "I haven't the time to pat their heads while they cry on my shoulder," said one. "Who needs it, anyway? It takes too much out of me. My men don't come to me with sob stories about how a buyer was rude to them, or made a pass at them." This man had never had women working for him, or he would not have talked like that. It is true that the manager of women does sometimes go home with his shirt collar damp with tears, but nobody ever promised him a rose garden, and tears don't stain. In any case this man is wrong. The successful woman in selling doesn't cry about the rudeness of buyers, and if one made a pass at her he could end up with an icy stare that froze him as solid as Lot's wife. The women I have met in business can take care of themselves.

Women come into the selling business because they are attracted by the higher incomes, because they want the freedom of action of a selling career, because they can't stand the routine of a desk job, or because they are not qualified for anything else—which are, of course, precisely the reasons men choose the selling business.

I have never felt the temptation to, as it were, draw a diagram of the archetypal successful salesman, but for some reason I do have a picture in my mind of the typical successful woman in the field. It is a potentially dangerous practice, this, but perhaps because I have met and worked with so many women who conform to the pattern, I can't get it out of my mind. If you look for this pattern in hiring women for your sales team, then don't blame me if it doesn't work—I said it was dangerous. Here she is:

She is in her late twenties or early thirties; probably divorced, separated or widowed; maybe some background in nursing, teaching, or commercial experience; not, repeat not, necessarily beautiful or even attractive to men but always immaculately groomed; poised and assured; articulate although not necessarily highly educated, and above all, determined to make it in a man's domain.

Certainly, women are different from men. They often need more assurance of worth, more recognition of effort, and more assistance with problems outside their day-to-day jobs. But if you play fair with them they can be capable of a fierce personal loyalty to you, they will respond willingly to an appeal for special effort, and they will show tremendous pride in the results of that effort. If you are a big enough man to induce this, then they will give it without hesitation or restraint.

All this is a great responsibility for a manager, and the truth is that most managers shrink from it, which is one reason we still hear all the old shibboleths about women in selling. Whichever way you feel, it's happening, so you might as well get used to the idea, and not only on your sales team: the next sales manager who sits behind your desk might well wear eye-shadow instead of after-shave.

WHO I THINK YOU ARE

Having said my piece on that subject, let me wind up this chapter by talking about you—whoever you are, whether male or female. The real reason for this book stems from the way you got your present job. Unless you are a very rare bird, you were promoted to the job of manager from the sales force. You were a salesman. Now, in almost every case, the people who pulled you up out of the ranks did so *not* because you were a potentially good manager but because you were the best *salesman* in the group. Senior managers do this all the time, and it is one of the commonest and silliest mistakes they make. They know perfectly well that the mere fact that someone is a good salesman is no indication that he will be a good manager. They even know that the opposite is often true—that those very characteristics which make him a good salesman can militate against his being a good manager—and yet they still do it. They promote the best salesman in the team and the result is often a double catastrophe; they lose a good salesman and gain a bad manager.

Why? Why are promotions from the ranks so often disastrous? The reason is simple and it is a great truth in business, but as with so many great truths it is often unrecognized or ignored. Here it is, and it is the most important thing in this introduction:

> *As a salesman, your value to the company depended entirely on your own performance. As a manager, your value depends entirely on the performance of others.*

Now a world-shattering announcement? But it is the basis of all good management, and the reason that many new managers fail in their jobs is that they have not understood this axiom, have not taken the mental leap from considering only *their* sales figures and *their* profitability to considering the sales figures and profitability of a team of salesmen.

So, your company promoted you to sales manager, and with one stroke they gave you a whole new set of problems, requiring a whole new set of skills—the skills of handling salesmen. The trouble is that these skills are not inherent in most of us; we don't bring them to the job; they must be *learned*.

Now the most effective way of learning is not through books or conferences or classrooms, it is through one's own experience. There can be no doubt about this; things learned by experience on the job, actually doing the work, are never forgotten. The reason experience is not practicable is that it takes too long and costs too much. Learning by experience means learning by making mistakes, and a manager of people makes *people* mistakes, which are very expensive mistakes indeed. Your top management is unlikely to look on patiently while you are learning through mistakes and, in the process, bringing your division to a grinding halt.

Therefore this book. It is intended to speed up the experience process of the new manager and to act as a refresher and guide to the more experienced man. I have kept it short so that you can read it at one sitting, and I suggest that you do just that. This will give you the highlights, so that when you have a problem in, say, staff selection, or you wish to set up an appraisal program or produce an incentive scheme, you can go back to that section and examine it more fully.

There is no bibliography in the end of the book. I have quoted from no authorities on management. The thoughts here are my own and they come from years of direct selling of everything from crawler tractors to baby bottles, from managing sales teams and from training salesmen and managers. I have invented no dramatically new management techniques or philosophies, nor do I espouse any of those currently in vogue. I have merely tried to get down in brief and easily readable form the job of a working sales manager. If what follows helps you in your job in any way at all—if you get only three workable ideas from these pages—then reading them will not have been a waste of time for you and I shall have done what I set out to do.

2

The Lonely Art of Leadership

When the ancient Greeks asked the Delphic Oracle for the root of all wisdom, the answer was, "Know thyself." Before we can manage people, before we can presume to affect the destinies of others, we need to take a long, hard look at ourselves. One of the most important questions a manager can ask himself is "What sort of manager am I?" Not, you will notice, "How good am I as a manager?" That comes much later. No, you have to know your management *style* long before you need to be worried about your management *ability*.

You are reading this book in the hope that it will better your ability, but your style you bring along with you; it is part of your make-up long before you ever became a manager. Where and how you acquired this style is a fascinating subject outside the scope of our inquiries, but depending on which school of psychology you favor, it came either from your great grandfather's chromosomes or from the fact that the boys picked on you when you were little because your ears stuck out.

Different managers manage in different ways. There is no single best way to manage people, just as there is no single best way to cook trout, swing an eight iron, or attack your opponent's king. It is necessary to examine the basic management philosophies in order to discover their strengths and weaknesses, to see where you fit into them, and to see how and why managers succeed—and fail.

If you have done any reading in management techniques—and there is so much of it around that it is difficult not to—you will have realized that sooner or later the writer succumbs to the temptation to put down a list of the characteristics of an ideal manager. It is presumptuous, but he almost always does it. Now if you recall any of these lists you will agree that while they are worded in different ways, they all have one thing in common. No single list contains one personality trait which we could call "bad"—every single item is a virtue. You never read that the compleat manager is tight with his money, hates small children, or sucks his teeth in public. No, if you believe these lists, then the successful manager is thoughtful, compassionate, sincere, tolerant, altruistic, recycles his bottles and cans, and is an all-round worthy citizen and a hell of a nice fellow.

The top manager may have these virtues, of course, just as a taxi driver or a helicopter pilot may have them, but they are not a necessary part of the job, and anyone who thinks they are probably thinks that Mary Poppins could actually fly.

Viscount Montgomery claimed that one of the prime characteristics of a leader is a high personal moral code. Now, you and I have known too many men who were hard-drinking, carousing, and generally hell-raising types and yet who were absolutely first-class manager of men to believe that this is true. The reason for Montgomery's stand here is simple: throughout his time as a military leader he himself was an ascetic, his own personal life was austere and above reproach, and he had fallen into the error of judging others by his own rather high standards. This is a common management fault. If you are, for example, a puritan yourself and you evaluate people by the standard of conduct you have set yourself, then you will spend your life in a completely futile struggle to change others to your own lifestyle. As a manager you will reject people because of it, and some of them will be very good people. You will accept other people because of it, and some of them will be quite useless to you.

Any manager may have the virtues of Francis of Assisi, and while these will ensure that he is a very good man they have absolutely nothing to do with his being a good manager. It's a hard, cold world out there, and you do not succeed as a manager because you are a sort of cross between a Salvation Army worker and a middle-aged boy scout. It doesn't happen that way.

Another necessary characteristics (according to the experts) is high intelligence. Few top managers are likely to deny this since it indicates, ipso facto, that they themselves are highly intelligent, and who is going to deny that he is intelligent? Nevertheless, it is not a vital management trait and let no one tell you that it is. I say this with complete confidence, not because I have read a hundred books on it but because my job keeps me in continual contact with top managers. I meet them all the time, and while I may admire and respect their achievements, this does not blind me to the fact that they do not have an IQ much above the people they manage. Indeed it is often the other way around; the worker is often more purely intelligent than his boss.

An intellectual is different from an intelligent person, of course, and here we are even further from the top manager. The truth is that the true intellectual has very little change of succeeding in management. If you read Kierkegaard or collect Bartok records or know all about the life and times of Savonarola, it's a safe bet that you won't ever reach the top rung. The big tycoons who buy post-impressionist art and finance avant-garde theatre do it after they have conquered their own personal Everests in business and, anyway, intellectual aspiration probably has nothing to do with their hobbies.

CHARACTERISTICS OF THE SUCCESSFUL MANAGER

Well, so far we have discussed what the successful manager is not. So what is he? Having been scornful of the people who compile lists of essential managerial characteristics, I expose myself to equal scorn by setting out one of my own. It is not exhaustive and it is certainly not intended to be the final say; these are simply some facets of character that I have noticed in successful managers.

1. He is selfish. Much further along, in the chapter on communication, we shall be examining loaded words, and "selfish" is certainly a loaded word. It has bad connotations. It conjures up unhappy feelings. Yet I say that the top manager is a selfish man, and I stand by the description. A dictionary definition of the word goes something like this: "Having regard for personal gain; actuated by or appealing to self-interest." That's him.

You don't like the idea? Think for a moment! A long time ago this man said to himself: "I want up. I want the things that go with a top executive position: the responsibility and authority, the respect of others, the air-conditioned limousine and the holidays in the Bahamas, the long hours, the hassles and the headaches of success. Now in order to attain this position I am prepared to make personal sacrifices. I am prepared to give up a lot of things which seem to be important now so that I can get the things which will be much more important to me in the future."

Now tell me—for whom is he making these sacrifices? For the good of mankind? For the good of his company? You know the answer—for *himself,* for himself and those close to him. "Actuated by or appealing to self-interest"—you know this is true.

When all the camouflage is stripped away, no manager ever does anything in business for the good of his company. He does it to protect, enlarge, reinforce, bolster, or ensure the survival of his job and therefore of himself. His interest in the company is *always* secondary to his own. If the owners of the company are intelligent, they acknowledge this and it doesn't bug them. They realize that the manager's worth to the company is that in almost all cases he can further his own interests only by furthering the company's, and they are prepared to live with this knowledge. I say "in almost all cases." Every now and then the manager realizes that his interests do not ride with those of the company and may even conflict with them, and he is then clearheaded enough to take immediate action to protect himself.

An example of this could be where a company is going through a depressed time; nobody's fault, the industry itself is in a recession. Now, while the company's best interests may be to pull in its horns and ride out the thin years, confident of an eventual resurging of the industry, the manager's best interests may be served by pulling out and entering a completely different industry. In such a case it would require a very sentimental personality to say, "The company has been good to me and I will not desert it in its hour of need!" The realist says, "The company has been good to me, but I have been good for the company. Those days are over and I am not going to sit becalmed in the middle of the ocean waiting for a breeze—I'm changing ships. Bye-bye, and wasn't it fun while it lasted?"

The top manager is selfish. If this word really worries you then call it self-centered or even egocentric—means the same thing, costs fifty cents more.

2. *He has direction.* I run my training clinics at all levels, from senior management all the way down to raw recruits, and even with these brand new boys I can sometimes say, "Harold won't make it, but Charles just might." What usually prompts these thoughts about Harold and Charles has nothing to do with their intelligence, their aptitude for learning, or even their degree of attention in the clinic. It is something which is sometimes hard to detect and which sometimes seems to envelop a man like an aura, and that something is a well-defined sense of direction. Not all of those who have this sense will succeed, but all of those who don't have it will fail.

I am not sure of many things, but I am sure of this. One outstanding characteristic of the successful manager, one thing which sets him above the rest of the herd, is the fact that he knows where he is going, how he intends to get there, and how long it will take him. He has direction, and this faculty alone is enough to take him a long way up the ladder of his choice.

All this is not to say that the direction he chooses early in life is the one he will follow throughout. It is rare indeed to find a man who has set his goals in high school and has clung to them without deviation. The point is that while he may change from time to time, he changes for reasons which seem good to him and him alone. He is flexible enough to change when it seems advisable, but *he* decides when and how.

I wish I had the eloquence to express this thought properly. The man who truly has direction is on the inside track in life, and his chances of success in any field he chooses are way ahead of the pack. The reason for this is simple, and it is a basic fact of life: *The world will always stand aside for a man who knows where he is going.* Most people don't know where they are going, and they respect and envy the man who does.

3. *He has empathy.* Empathy is a much-used word in discussions on management, and most people use it wrongly. It has nothing to do with sympathy, although it is often used as an alternative or synonym for it. Sympathy is a warm emotion; empathy is a clinical talent. Empathy is the ability to project your own personality into

the person or situation you are considering and thereby to understand that person or situation completely.

I apologize for getting a little didactical about the word, but if it is a prime characteristic of a manager then we need to know exactly what we are talking about. Yes, the successful manager has empathy. The faculty is well developed in him. It leads to people saying that he is highly intelligent (not necessarily true), that he is perceptive, that he can read people, that he can get to the heart of a problem.

I don't know how deeply to go into the subject of empathy, because although it certainly is one of the most important aspects of the top manager's make-up, it is not something which you can learn. There are no correspondence courses in empathy, you can't get it at a university course, and you certainly won't get it in one of my management clinics—even if I could give it to you I don't have any to spare. If you don't have this talent it is only fair to tell you that you will probably never be a truly great manager of men.

That is being honest with you. I could pretend either that it isn't all that important or that you can learn to be empathetic. It is, and you can't.

All truly great racing drivers have a weird sort of sense known as *proprioception*. It is a highly developed awareness of where one is in relation to other things. The driver can come out of a fast bend at 150 miles an hour, hit an oil slick, and spin down the track, apparently completely out of control. Yet coming out of the eighth complete revolution, moving at a mere 70 miles an hour, he can point the car in precisely the right direction, slam it into gear, and be in business again. The point is that through all that incredible gyrating he knows exactly where he is in relation to the road. You can't learn proprioception, which is why there are so few great racing drivers. You can't learn empathy, which is why there are so few great managers.

If this sounds depressing, if you feel that you don't have any marked talent for empathy, you need not despair. You can still be a competent manager. I was never a great manager because I don't have very much empathy; I am simply not interested enough in people. Nevertheless I made a good living and ran a successful team without it. Don't ever forget that in this life you are judged, not by how good you are, but by how much better you are than those around you, and since very, very few managers have high empathy you can still do well, and look good, by comparison.

4. *He is a lonely man.* Look around you at the general run of managers and this point seems crazy. A manager lonely? Why, surely the very reverse is true! Yet it is so. Remember that the characteristics we are examining are those of the top managers, the créme de la créme, the elite.

They are lonely men. They have hundreds of acquaintances but few really close friends. I suppose that it is more accurate to say that they are "alone" men rather than "lonely" men, since the word "lonely" suggests the wish to be with people, whereas the top man values his private times, his private places.

One reason for this aloneness is a minor tragedy, in a way. What has happened is that the successful manager has grown away from the friends of his early days and has no common ground on which to meet them any more. This happens all the time, of course. Your successful sales manager was once a salesman himself, he was part of that happy, noisy bunch of drummers who laughed, played, drank, and sold together. Now he is establishment, and the sales team, that happy, noisy bunch—now older, quieter, and no longer quite so happy—are still salesmen.

This is one of the personal sacrifices the manager realized that he would have to make, that if he intended to rise above the faceless ones he would lose their close friendship—not that he would drop them, merely that they would drift apart. Even when he was part of the team, he was never the noisiest or happiest, not by choice but because of the sort of person he is.

Generalizations are often dangerous, but here is one you may care to ponder: The clown of the group never gets promoted. Everybody loves old Charlie and he is a real wow at the office party, but he never seems to move out of the ruck. As the years go by he stays in the ranks, the jokes a little thinner, the laugh a little strained, as he wonders what the hell happened to his luck.

5. *He believes.* It may seem that the picture I have drawn so far is the picture of a rather unpleasant person—selfish, clinical, lonely, humorless. It may be so in some cases, but this last aspect may soften the outline a little.

Our top man is able to *communicate* with people in a way that most of us cannot. He communicates not only instructions, ideas, and information but also moods, attitudes, and feelings. Why is he so good at this? Is it a special talent he has, in the same way that he has empathy?

It is not a special talent, but it is something he has—it is belief. *He believes in what he is doing.* He believes that his job is worthwhile, valuable, valid, and right. Skeptical he may be and often is, *but he is not a hypocrite,* and because he believes he is able to communicate this belief to others.

The picture is sometimes painted of the top executive as a sort of Svengali or puppet-master, cynically pulling the strings to activate his men and chuckling evilly as they dance to his tune. This may have been the picture in the days of the Great Depression, when such concepts as Human Relations and Motivation were considered unnecessary luxuries (if, indeed, any manager gave them a moment's thought), but the picture is no longer valid, nor has it been for many years.

In those days a man worked as hard as he could in the worst conditions and for the lowest pay, simply to keep his job and fill the bellies of his children. He was motivated by the terror of losing that job and the knowledge that a hundred men were standing in line, eager to take over whenever his manager had the idea that he was not doing his utmost.

Those days are gone, thank God, and now we have to manage by communicating with our people. The top manager communicates well because he believes, and because he believes he is able to set the hearts of his men on fire. They believe because he believes; his belief shines out of him and transmits itself to his team. The whole essence of true communication in management is right here. The hypocritical manager never really gets through to his people. The old saying that you can fool the people above you but you can't fool the people below you is as true now as it has ever been.

TEST YOUR LEADERSHIP PATTERN

So much for this rare bird, the successful top manager. It is broad and elementary, but it will serve as a foundation on which we can stand to take a closer look at management styles. We are going to do that in a moment, but before we do, please find a pencil and complete the little leadership pattern quiz. Don't read on, fill it in right now, or the point of it will be lost. Some thoughts to bear in mind as you do it:

There are no right answers or wrong answers. You cannot fail this quiz, you cannot pass it.

Answer only "yes" or "no"—you have to plump for one or the other. No maybe's or perhaps's or possibly's.

This is not a test of your *ability* as a manager; it is an attempt to discover your *style* of leadership.

Don't try to outguess the question because there are no trick questions.

Don't ask yourself which the "best" answer would be. Simply put down the answer which conforms to your own pattern.

Answer according to the way you are now, not the way you would like to be.

The question may not apply to your present job; even so, it must be answered. Ask yourself, "if it did apply to my job, what would my answer be?"

Off you go.

1. Do your men have in their possession a detailed job discription which you have discussed with them?

    YES ☐ NO ☐

2. At a staff meeting, do your people expect you to do most of the talking? YES ☐ NO ☐

3. Do your immediate subordinates address you as "Mr." or stand when you enter the room? YES ☐ NO ☐

4. Do you believe that the future of your men depends largely on your present leadership of them? YES ☐ NO ☐

5. If it were possible, would you talk to each of your men every day about their day-to-day work? YES ☐ NO ☐

6. Do you believe that a written memo is a more effective way of passing on instructions than a discussion?

    YES ☐ NO ☐

7. Do you generally avoid going to parties to which you have been invited at the homes of your staff? YES ☐ NO ☐

8. Do you disagree with the philosophy that "a happy team is an efficient team"?   YES ☐ NO ☐

9. Do you know fairly accurately where each one of your team will be and what they will be doing throughout today?
                                                      YES ☐ NO ☐

10. Does your team accept your ideas and instructions without needing to talk them over with you?   YES ☐ NO ☐

11. Do your people generally make an appointment to see you, rather than walk into your office without notice?
                                                      YES ☐ NO ☐

12. When tackling a project, is getting the job done more on your mind than the personalities of the people involved?
                                                      YES ☐ NO ☐

13. Do you regularly spend time with each man watching him at work and/or working with him at his job? YES ☐ NO ☐

14. Do you keep a fairly firm hand on meetings, discouraging any arguments across the table?   YES ☐ NO ☐

15. At a staff party, would your presence at your team's table have a quietening effect on their fun and games?
                                                      YES ☐ NO ☐

16. Tomorrow you have to reprimand one of your men. Do you know that you will be in complete command of the interview, even though he is a strong and outspoken personality?   YES ☐ NO ☐

BASIC MANAGEMENT PATTERNS

Now that you have answered the quiz, leave it for a moment. We are now going to do something which admittedly can be dangerous, and that is to tie labels to people and slot them neatly into pigeonholes. Any student of mankind knows that this can be a perilous practice. People are highly complex mechanisms and we take grave risks when we try to categorize them.

Nevertheless, and conceding that we are oversimplifying a complicated task, we have to start somewhere. Here then are the basic management patterns.

THE STRONG/HARD MANAGER

There are a lot of long words we could use to describe this man—despotic, authoritative, dictatorial, take your pick. I prefer simply to call him *hard*. Now, there must be no misunderstanding here. The word "hard" is not a criticism or comment of any kind, it is merely a *description* of the management philosophy.

The Strong/Hard leader is a "thing" person rather than a "people" person. He is oriented towards the job rather than the people who do the job. He makes most of the decisions himself, relays them to the staff in the form of fiats or instructions, and confidently expects them to be carried out without question. He does not need discussion about the instruction from his men; all he wants is efficient and instant obedience. The people under him may have titles and positions, but they have very little authority to act on their own, to develop their own ideas, or to make their own decisions.

I recall talking to the financial director of a company a few years ago. He was something of a wiz-kid, having become director at the age of twenty-nine. I asked him how things were going, and he astonished me by saying that he had left his company and had joined a much smaller crowd.

I asked, "What on earth made you give up the job of financial director?" He said, "Michael, I was never the financial director. I was an accounting clerk with my name on the letterhead. I couldn't even pass a requisition for carbon paper without clearing it with the boss." This mans's Boss was Strong/Hard.

Now it is easy to heap scorn on the Strong/Hard manager because his faults and weaknesses are obvious. Be careful, though, before you reject this philosophy outright, because the Strong/Hard man has a lot of things going for him which we can admire. Here are a few:

In the first place he is *personally competent*. He knows his job. If you are going to make all the decisions yourself then those decisions had better be right or you won't have a job.

Secondly, he is not afraid to assume the mantle of power and responsibility. Many people who would like to have the trappings and symbols of authority have no great wish to expose themselves to the risks that go with them. A cold wind blows up there at the top of the mountain; it's a lot cosier down here. The Strong/Hard manager is not afraid of the wind. He is the boss. He confidently accepts the risks.

Another thing which clearly distinguishes him is his capacity for getting through a lot of work in a very short time. This is partly because the decisions he makes are the decisions of one man. He doesn't find it necessary to call a conference every time he wants to buy a pair of socks, and this makes him an efficient user of time.

He also provides something which is so often lacking in many business organizations, namely, *a clearly defined focus of power*. Under such a man, people know exactly what their limits of authority and responsibility are, and while these may be very restricted, at least there is no way a man can say to himself; "What can I or can't I do? How far am I allowed to take this? What exactly is my job anyway?"

This point is important and worth expanding. Investigations seem to show that while people work best within wide limits of responsibility with clearly defined boundaries, and that they work worst with narrow limits of responsibility with ill-defined boundaries, they can also work amazingly well within narrow limits—so long as these limits are well defined. The Strong/Hard man understands this. He doesn't give his people much latitude to make their own decisions about things but at least they know exactly what that latitude is. He provides strong, confident, consistent leadership.

Do not misunderstand if I compare this with the training of a thoroughbred show dog, because the analogy is valid enough. The happiest dog is the one who knows precisely what is expected of it; its limits of action are well-defined and constant. If you want to see a really confused Afghan hound then come around to the Beer household. The sloppy way we have reared our dearly loved pet means that from one day to the next she doesn't know whether or not she is allowed to chase bicycles or sleep on our bed. She has had no consistent and well-defined guidance on these matters.

Lastly, in an emergency or crisis the Strong/Hard manager really comes into his own. If there were no competition in business, if a company could be run as a scout camp, there would be no need for this man. But since most companies seem to progress from one crisis to another, where quick, decisive action is required, there will always be a place for him.

There are a few—a very few—men who could be called the professional managers. They are called in when a company which has been operating satisfactorily finds that it has stopped growing or has started going downhill. Let us say that such a company is in the business of manufacturing and selling alkahests. In desperation the owners of the company call in a professional manager (if you like, a doctor of sick businesses) to straighten things out.

Now this man knows nothing whatever about alkahests; what he does know is how to apply the kiss of life to an organization which has gone into Cheyne-Stokes breathing. He examines the situation and says something like this: "Right. I am dispensing with the Public Relations Department immediately; if the PR man wants to stay with us he can work in shipping, Weinstein and Rogers go up to board level. We are getting into television advertising to the tune of half a million. Tell the manager of the eastern factory that I want it closed down by August. From next week we are going to stop making liquid alkahests and concentrate on solids only. Make Acme Alkahests an offer of seven million for 51 percent of their company."

There is an outraged scream from three department heads, eleven people resign, he gets two anonymous threatening letters, there is a secret protest meeting at the home of the product manager for liquid alkahests, our professional manager's coffee begins to taste oddly bitter—and the company begins once again to prosper. Do you see what is meant by calling him a "thing" person rather than a "people" person? And of course he writes his own ticket—there is no limit to what such a man is worth.

It will be clear that I have a good deal of admiration for the Strong/Hard man. Certainly he has weaknesses. He rides roughshod over the sensitivities of others, he allows no criticisms of his decisions, he does not (and this is his most grievous fault) build people under him, so that when he leaves there is no one to take his place. All this is true. But when the dam has burst and everyone is running for his life, it is this man who tells everyone which way to run. It is usually the right way.

The archetype of this school of leadership was probably Charles de Gaulle. Here was a man who made all his own decisions. Try to think of a strong personality in French politics during de Gaulle's term of office and you find that you can't. France was de Gaulle and de Gaulle was France. His foreign minister, his United Nations representative, his finance minister (a brilliant man), what were they but the mouthpieces of their boss? They could not make the smallest decisions on their own, and if they dared to air their own opinions publicly, the voice from on high cut them down—publicly. During the eleven years that he ruled France he antagonized individuals and nations, and it is not too much to say that at one time he was the most disliked man in the free world.

What can we put on the other side of the scale? Only this—that he did the job he was hired to do. When he was asked to take over again, France, considered as a viable political structure, was a sort of international joke. The French were used to having one government before breakfast and another one after lunch. Charles de Gaulle put his country back in business. With all his faults, his terrible blind spots, the Strong/Hard manager *gets the job done.*

THE WEAK/HARD MANAGER

The second philosophy of leadership is a character we can call the Weak/Hard manager. He is easily recognized by his two-faced attitude: he kow-tows to his superiors and cracks the whip at those under him. Do not confuse him with the Strong/Hard man because they are poles apart. The Strong/Hard manager is a *strong* personality who *dominates;* the Weak/Hard is a *weak* personality who *domineers.* His fundamental problem is one of insecurity. The veneer of toughness is paper thin, and under it there is a quaking and terrified beast. This is somewhat true of all of us, of course, but his veneer is thinner than most.

I have put the case for the Strong/Hard manager rather forcefully because at his best he can be very effective, but there isn't one good thing we can say for the Weak/Hard manager. He is the typical empire-builder in his company. When Shakespeare said: "Man, proud man, drest in a little brief authority . . .," he was looking straight at a Weak/Hard manager.

Because he is afraid of people, afraid that they might catch him up and pass him, the Weak/Hard manager hires people in his own image. Now in fact we all do this and it is one of the worst mistakes we make in staff selection, but this man carries it to an extreme. He hires pale shadows of himself, people with the built-in flaws of the petty dictator. We can call this "the carbon-copy syndrome," and it leads to multiplication of inefficiency. The Weak/Hard manager is an ideal bureaucrat, and you will find him in government departments all over the world.

If he has no redeeming feature, if he merely fills space without enriching it, why mention the Weak/Hard man at all? Good question, but we are examining managers both good and bad, so that we can recognize them when we come round a rock and meet them face to face. There is an amazing number of Weak/Hard managers around, and the big puzzle is how they got there in the first place. Nepotism raises its familiar face, of course, but there isn't so much of that these days. Nigel doesn't automatically go into the family business and, after a gruelling training period of three weeks, find himself on the board. Few companies can afford to carry passengers in these tightly competitive times, and Nigel's uncles are more likely to hire a Strong/Hard man and suggest to Nigel that he study botany in the Amazon basin.

Last thoughts about this character before we forget him and turn to grownups again: he has probably reached his peak of promotion. The Weak/Hard man is not readily promotable material, and let us offer up a small prayer of thanks that this is so.

THE TRUE/SOFT MANAGER

Again, please remember that the word "soft" implies no praise and no criticism—it is only a description. I wish there were words to describe these leadership patterns which were completely neutral. There are none, and although I should like to be able to make up words to fit, I am not up to Humpty Dumpty's skill in general semantics.

The True/Soft manager is, at first sight, the ideal manager. He is a people person. He encourages and even demands participation in decision making. He is vitally concerned with building people, making them bigger and better and more valuable to the company and to themselves, helping them to grow. He works by using the "committee decision" technique very extensively; it is a way of life for him. For example, if there is a top-level decision to be made, he will not make it on his own—in his organization there is a standing committee composed of senior management to do this. Equally, down the line in the company hierarchy the same thing happens.

The district supervisor with three salesmen under him will bring them in on any discussion of changing their territories, rather than changing them on his own account and handing down the decision as a fait accompli.

This is all very well and good, and the True/Soft man has a very good chance of being a highly successful manager. Before we get too cosy about him however, let us concede that just as the Strong/Hard man with all his faults has some very fine things going for him, so the True/Soft man with all his obvious good qualities has problems which stem from his particular philosophy.

His first problem is one of *time*. Consider it: He has created an organization in which participation in decision making has been drummed into his people. They have been taught to expect that they will be brought into the inner circle on questions which affect them, and this means anything from whether to build a new factory complex to what type of coffee machine should be installed in the order department.

Now suddenly this manager finds himself in an emergency situation. Quick, decisive action is needed. What does he do? He can do one of two things, both of which could bring trouble. If he makes the decision himself because of the urgency, he may confuse and antagonize his people, who have come to expect that their ideas will always be solicited. On the other hand, if he calls his meeting and has the usual confab about the situation, then the opportunity may have passed—or the danger erupted—before the committee has been able even to draft an agenda, let alone make a decision.

Here's another situation which can plague the True/Soft man. Let us suppose that there are two possible paths towards a certain goal and that our manager has decided that path X is the right one. He has based his decision on his long experience of similar problems and his considered assessment of all available information. He knows, as well as anyone can know, that he is right. He puts the situation to his group and they, to his astonishment and horror, choose path Y. They are unanimous about it and are confident that they are right, and none of his careful explanations of the other point of view has the slightest effect. Respectfully (he is, after all, their superior) but firmly they stick to their guns.

Now what the hell is he to do? Does he go along with them towards what he is certain will be disaster, or does he tear off his all-pals-together mask, produce the whip, and turn into a sort of son of Ivan the Terrible? If he does, he will never again be completely trusted by his men.

This may be digressing a little, but if you ever intend switching your basic leadership pattern, then do remember that it is very much easier to go from Hard to Soft than the other way about. A long time ago in a large international company I was offered a big promotion to a subsidiary of the firm outside the country. (I was offered the job because the two men above me had turned it down.) I was flattered but apprehensive, because it meant that I would be in charge of a division of fifteen people, all of them strangers to me and most of them probably antagonistic because they had hoped for the job themselves.

I voiced my fears to my boss before I left to take over. He said, "Michael, don't worry about the technical side of the job—that you can do quite easily. On the people side, take my advice: don't try to be too friendly too soon. Aim to have your staff saying to each other in six months' time that maybe you aren't quite the swine they thought you were going to be when you first came." Overstated, perhaps, but valuable advice to a novice manager.

A last thought on the True/Soft manager. Of all management types he is the one who needs the most patience and tolerance. His job will take more out of him emotionally than any other management pattern.

THE FALSE/SOFT MANAGER

I hate this man.

I hate him because he is dishonest, and while being dishonest about things is not good, being dishonest about people is very bad indeed. He is dishonest because by nature and inclination he is Hard but he hides this behind a facade of Soft. He goes through the motions of participative management without for a moment believing in the people-philosophy of the True/Soft man. He asks his team for ideas, but he has no intention of ever adopting these ideas: He invites decisions but somehow they are always shelved.

He is a shabby creature, this character, and it would give me great pleasure to be able to say that he is always ineffective in his job. By any criterion he should be, but I have seen False/Soft men do a surprizingly competent job. I myself actually worked under one for a time, and under him the department prospered and grew. Probably the reason for this is that the False/Soft man is, after all, a Hard manager, and he carries with him the powerful weapons of the Hard man, even though he conceals these under a Soft cloak.

What does happen to him, I am delighted to record, is that he often has a high turnover of staff. People will forgive a manager many things, but they resent being taken for fools, and you can't play the False/Soft game for too long before people realize that their opinions carry no weight, that they are in fact only a chorus line supporting the star. When this man's staff see him for what he is, there is often a rush for the door—and the pity of it is that it is the bright boys, the managers of tomorrow, who leave.

This is an appropriate time for a word of warning. We are discussing the techniques of handling people; the whole book is devoted to this. Somewhere through this book you may decide to use certain of these techniques yourself, but beware. To be effective in the long term you must *believe* what you do. The manager who cynically uses a technique without a true belief and an honest intent is going to find that it eventually blows up in his face. Let me repeat something: the successful manager is not a hypocrite. Cold-eyed, hard-nosed, even disillusioned sometimes, but not hypocritical. An odd tenet of faith from someone who, because he has spent a lot of his life training managers, should be more cynical than most? Not at all, and every management clinic I run confirms this belief. The good ones—the ones who are going to make it right to the top—they *believe*.

And there are your four management styles. Astonishing, really, that there are only four. You may have read books or articles which mention a dozen or more, but anything else is merely an offshoot from one of these styles. The truth is even simpler: there are actually only two management philosophies. They are, of course, Hard and Soft, and everything else in management stems from one of these.

You will have realized that we have been looking at caricatures. The 100 percent Hard or 100 percent Soft manager does not occur in nature, just as there is no living creature with 100 percent male or female hormones. We have caricatured them deliberately, made them larger than life, in order to examine them more easily.

THE IDEAL MANAGER

After all this there is still another management style. I have no label to tie to this one, so find one of your own that suits. This manager recognizes two things about his job. First, he recognizes that a business entity is not a democracy. Management is not elected by popular vote; it is placed in power through the arbitrary decision of a small group of people who are themselves in positions of power. The man so placed is given the job so that he can use the power, and his electors expect him to act like a manager. Certain decisions are made by him alone; he cannot delegate them, and he cannot abdicate his position of responsibility. Thus the straight Soft philosophy is simply not on.

Second, in spite of the above, he knows that people need to grow, need to contribute, need to assume power right up to their level of ability. Therefore he realizes that the pure Hard road does not lead to a viable long-term management system and he rejects it. He holds to himself the responsibility for decisions which are his by right of command, but he passes on those which can be handled by capable people under him. He is a mixture of the best aspects of Hard and Soft.

I was talking recently with the sales director of one of my client companies and I asked him how he would describe himself as a manager. "Oh, I'm a hard-driving swine," he said, and he wasn't smiling. "I expect the utmost from my men at all times. I set high targets and when my salesmen reach them I make them even higher."

"Would you work for you?"

"Never!" And he still wasn't smiling.

I asked whether he had a high staff turnover and he shook his head. "Men don't leave this company much. Sometimes the company leaves them, but not the other way around." He showed me his figures, and the annual turnover of his sales staff was less than 6 percent. Compared with the much-quoted figure of 15 percent this was excellent, and I wondered why his men stayed with him if he was such a slave driver.

I stopped wondering when I attended one of his monthly sales meetings. He opened the meeting by standing up and talking for less than twenty minutes. He gave out a few instructions, showed the group a new promotional piece and mentioned one or two particularly good performances by some of the salesmen. Then he sat down and *his salesmen took over that meeting*. They discussed points, they agreed, they argued. They asked him for his opinion and disagreed with him when he gave it. They wandered off the subject, they often had three people talking at the same time, they violated every rule of debate in the book. In the process they had a meeting which was stimulating, fruitful, and morale building. At the end they surged out of the conference room as though they were ready to take on the four horsemen of the Apocalypse.

I realized that their manager was a classic example of the best mixture of Hard and Soft. On the one hand he ran his team hard, setting high standards and demanding excellent and consistent performance. On the other, he recognized their right to question, to contribute, to share in decision making about the things which affected them.

I suppose that this is near to an ideal manager. He need not operate in exactly this way. Indeed it could be the kiss of death for some managers to let their sales team take over a meeting as this one did. Nevertheless, that is the pattern of a successful manager. He knows that he can get an astonishing amount of effort from a man so long as that man has some say in how, where, and when the effort is applied.

YOUR OWN MANAGEMENT STYLE

And now you are ready to discover your own personal management philosophy. Go back to the quiz and check it with the numbers below.

S	C	A	P
1	2	3	4
5	6	7	8
9	10	11	12
13	14	15	16

Totals:

The numbers under S, C, A, and P correspond with the numbers of the sixteen questions in the quiz. Circle those numbers where you answered "Yes" to the question. Now total up the number of rings in each column and write that number at the bottom of each column. For example, if in column S you circled 5 and 13, the total for column S is 2.

YOUR LEADERSHIP PATTERN

Supervision	Communication	Attitude	Personality
CLOSE	DIRECTIVE	REMOTE	DOMINANT
4	4	4	4
3	3	3	3
2	2	2	2
1	1	1	1
0	0	0	0
FREE	PERMISSIVE	AMIABLE	COMPLIANT

Now look at the table headed "Your Leadership Pattern" and transfer your totals to the pattern by circling the relevant number in each of the four columns. For example, if your totals for columns S, C, A, and P were 1, 2, 4, and 1 respectively, you would circle 1 under Supervision, 2 under Communication, 4 under Attitude, and 1 under Personality. Join the ringed numbers with straight lines as you would a child's join-the-dots puzzle, and you are in business. Using the example above, the resulting chart would look like this:

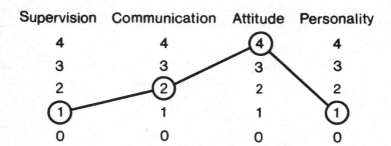

Now that you have what I call your "SCAP" pattern down on paper, what does it mean? Remember, first of all, that the marks show only the *type* of leadership—they are no indication of *ability* as a leader. So, suppose you have a 4 under the Supervision column; this means that you supervise your team very closely indeed—you practically breathe down their necks while they are doing their jobs. A 0 in that column, on the other hand, means that you run them on a very long leash, with little actual supervision. A 3 means fairly close supervision, 1 means fairly free: 2 is the neutral number throughout the four columns, with no leaning either way.

Under Communication, a 4 mark means that you don't communicate as much as you simply hand down instructions. A 0 is right across the other side of the scale—you almost never give outright instructions, you ask for their opinions instead. Again, 3 is fairly directive, 1 is fairly permissive, 2 is neutral.

Same thing under Attitude. A 4 means that you are very remote (this is at the personal, not the business level). Not *hostile,* of course, merely remote. And 0 means that you are a "buddy' type of manager, very amiable and social.

The Personality column is a shade more subtle. A mark of 4 does not necessarily mean a strong personality, just as a mark of 0 does not mean a weak one. What the numbers signify is the *degree* of personality which you bring into your dealings with people. You may have a very strong personality which you do not, as it were, bring to work with you, and in this case your mark could be 2, 1, or even (although this is unlikely) 0. If a good deal of you, not as a manager but as a *person,* comes through when handling people, then your mark would be 3 or 4.

Now add your four totals together to get a grand total. If this is between 10 and 16 then you are a Hard manager; the nearer to 16, the harder you are. If you are between 6 and 0 then you are a Soft manager; the nearer to 0, the softer you are. Remember again that no praise or blame is intended by use of the words "hard" or "soft." You can be a very good (or very bad) manager with a straight 4-4-4-4 SCAP pattern just as you can with a 0-0-0-0 pattern.

No, come to think of it, that isn't quite right. While it is true that your SCAP pattern is neither good nor bad by itself, any very high or very low pattern—that is, very hard or very soft—may mean that you are simply too inflexible to adjust to different leadership requirements, and that is one of the reasons for analyzing yourself by means of this pattern.

I conceived the SCAP pattern for two reasons first, because before we can even begin to handle people we should know what type of managers we are, and second, knowing our pattern helps us to realize that there will be times when we have to change it deliberately in order to be able to deal with a special situation. For example, you may be a 1 or 0 under Attitude; you prefer to run your team on a somewhat informal and social level. Fine, but what if one of your men is himself a very friendly type, to the extent that the relationship between you is in danger of turning into a mutual admiration society? You might feel that in this case you should adopt a more formal, remote attitude to prevent a loss of authority The key word here is *flexibility*—the willingness to adapt your natural management philosophy to meet different situations.

Now that you know what type of manager you are according to the SCAP pattern, do you agree with it, or do you feel that the pattern is wrong for you? When I dreamed up this method of defining management philosophy many years ago I put myself through the quiz as the first guinea pig, and I was surprised to find that it made me out to be harder than I thought I was. I had always thought of myself as a very easy-going, informal, permissive, and amiable manager, and according to my SCAP pattern I wasn't. I mentioned this to one or two people who had known me in the days when I was running a team of salesmen, and they were embarrassingly quick to confirm the results of the test. One of them had been on my sales team and he scoffed at the idea that I had been easy going. "If one of us ever put a foot wrong you used to chop us up into bite-sized pieces and eat us raw," he commented. Oh, well.

A well-known and highly respected method of defining management styles draws a graph which claims to tell you whether your management practice is good or bad, weak or strong, according to how you answer certain questions. I don't aim as high as this because I don't believe that you can judge a manager's *competence* by getting him to answer questions on a piece of paper. All I aim for in the SCAP pattern is to indicate *how* you go about your job, not how *well* you do it. In the last analysis there is only one way to judge management ability and that is to watch the manager at work. All we have done here is to obey the Oracle at Delphi—"Know thyself, it is the beginning of wisdom "

3

The Subtle Art of Remuneration

Few discussions on how to handle salesmen end without some mention of remuneration, so important is it. Yet it is not often realized that the type of salesman we attract to our companies depends largely on the remuneration we offer; not only on how much we pay them, but also *how* we pay them, and there is a world of difference between *how much* and *how*. Let's first take a look at how much.

HOW MUCH TO PAY?

The simplest way to pay a salesman, or indeed anyone who works for you, is to calculate with demoniacal shrewdness exactly how little it takes to keep him with you. Ten cents less and he will leave, ten cents more and you are overpaying him. Setting aside the ethical aspects of this philosophy (which we could call the Scrooge syndrome), it fails because it depends on a variable, and that is the state of the labor market. If there is full employment of salesmen because of a buoyant economy, you will have to pay more; if there is general unemployment you can pay peanuts. The trouble is that this situation changes, sometimes dramatically, from year to year, and you can hardly have your salary scale going up and down like a yo-yo. Forget it. The only men you will attract with this type of remuneration plan will be those who can't get a job elsewhere. You will deserve them.

Then there is the "replacement value" concept, namely, if he left me, what would it cost to replace him? Many managers will assert

32

that they work on this method, and most of them are lying; they don't. On the face of it, this is the most fair and reasonable way to pay. How can you knock it? A man is worth what it would cost to get an identical replacement for him, surely? End of story, it would seem, but it doesn't work like that.

In the first place you can almost never get an identical replacement because there is no such animal. You can get a salesman who may be able to sell as well or even better, but you still haven't replaced the man who has left because you have lost depth product knowledge, experience of working with your company's policies and procedures, relationships with customers, familiarity with territory, and, as they say in the advertisements, much, much more. If your new man is worth his salt he will eventually absorb all this, but it takes time.

Secondly, for some reason which nobody has ever satisfactorily explained, the remount always costs more than the original horse. A man with similar ability, potential, and experience won't look at the job unless it pays higher than it did. When you think of it, the explanation is not so esoteric. Your original man probably left you for more money, and the replacement will also probably only leave his present job for more money. All right, I said "probably." Of course, there are many other reasons, but when you get down to bedrock, it is an increase in income which accounts for most staff movement, and you better believe it. If increased income accounts for most sales personnel changes, does it not mean that all salesmen are being paid too little? Not at all (although your sales team would argue this to hell and back again)—it is simply a fact of life.

The reason that the replacement value idea is unsound, no matter what managers may say to the contrary, is exactly the same reason that the Scrooge syndrome won't work—it depends on the labor market. In bad times replacement salaries are low and in good times they are astronomical, and once this axiom is accepted it quickly appears that the two methods—the obviously nasty Scrooge syndrome and the apparently humanitarian replacement value idea— are in fact based on the same concept: what do I *have* to pay?

The third system, and we are on cloud nine here because so few companies seem to work to this idea, is to take an honest look at the job itself. What level of man do we need? How much experience must he have? What qualifications are required, and how long has he had to work to attain these? Do I want a man who can one day sit in my chair? How much does he have to take home each month to give him a certain personal dignity? To relieve him of financial problems so that he can attack his job with all his heart? What level of income does it need to give him pride when he tells his wife about it? (You don't think that's important? Put yourself in his place for a moment!)

Cloud nine, indeed, but if management went mad and adopted this system as a way of life there would be a change in attitude in their people which would pass belief.

Many managers take an interesting attitude towards payment of salesmen which at first sight is the most logical of all—they pay on the salesman's profitability. We are not talking about paying commission on sales, simply that the salesman's salary is geared to some fraction of what we have come to expect from that man and his territory. It is a pity that this won't work, because it really is simple, but the fact is that far from being logical it is completely illogical and impracticable. You may have two salesmen, Phillips and Howard, and Phillips is bringing in twice as much sales volume as Howard. However, the true picture is that Phillips is skimming the cream off a highly profitable territory, while Howard is scraping every cent in sales out of a tough territory against the strongest opposition. The idea of paying by profitability in this case is ludicrous.

Having made that last point, there is another point to be made which could change your entire thinking about the remuneration of salesmen. Let us say that you have one salesman who, while the territories are all pretty much the same in potential and geography, nevertheless consistently outsells every other salesman on your team by two to one:

	Phillips	The Rest
Monthly sales:	50,000	25,000

Hah, we say; Phillips is worth any two of the other salesmen. Is that so? In this company of ours we make around 10 percent profit:

	Phillips	The Rest
Monthly sales:	50,000	25,000
10% profit:	5,000	2,500

A simple calculation, which seems to confirm that Phillips is worth twice as much as any other salesman. But wait a minute. *What does it cost us to keep any one single salesman on the road?* More than his salary—much more. His car, expense account, pension fund, medical insurance must be added to what you pay him. If his supervisor has five men reporting to him, then one-fifth of all the supervisor's expenses must be added on, and so on. In our example, it is by no means too much to say at least 2,000 (dollars, rubles, rands, whatever) a month per salesman—no matter how high or low his sales figures are:

	Phillips	The Rest
10% profit:	5,000	2,500
Cost per salesman:	−2,000	−2,000
Net profit:	3,000	500

Now what does it look like? Phillips worth twice as much as any other salesman? He is worth *six times* as much!

And I can hear the angry roar of the accountants hot on my trail to dispute my figures. Don't bother; I'm not interested. I know that they are oversimplified and that this is an amateurish way of looking at the position. The point is still there, and although you can argue until nightfall, the point remains. Your real crackerjack salesman is worth more than you are paying him now, unless you are already paying him well above the average of your "average" salesmen.

COMPLACENCY PLATEAUS

Here is another thought to make the problem of how much to pay your salesmen even more of a headache. I call it the "Complacency Plateau." Every one of us—you, me, Charlie over there—has a monthly or yearly level expressed in terms of plain money which represents the minimum amount required to provide what we consider to be the basic necessities of gracious living. It is a different level for each of us because our basic necessities are different. For Charlie the necessity may simply be that of providing food and shelter for his family. For me, the absolute basics may be sufficient Johnnie Walker and golf balls to make life bearable. For you, the talking begins with a yacht anchored off the Costa Brava. However high or low it may be, we each have our own level. Now, we will work hard to reach this level, and the motivation is simple, being a plain money requirement.

Fine so far, but then we reach our Complacency Plateau, and what happens? You *know* what happens: We level off and (take note, this is the point) you cannot get extra work from us by offering extra money. Our values change. "Hell, no!" the salesman says. "How many meals can I eat in a day? I have some money in the bank, we live in a nice house, our children are in good schools, we have two cars, a swimming pool, and a membership at the country club. I work hard enough as it is." He will not refuse more money if you stuff it into his ear, but don't expect proportionately more work from him—he has reached his Complacency Plateau.

The plateau is not constant, of course; it varies as his circumstances change. But the whole point of the Complacency Plateau is:

> *Money, beyond a certain level, is an ineffective motivator of people.*

Were this not true, then every commission salesman would be a millionarie because he would never stop selling. It *is* true, and after a certain level he *does* stop selling. Any manager of commission salesmen knows that this is true because his sales graphs tell him so. Once Charlie has reached a certain commission level for the month he eases off—he has reached his level of complacency. An acknowledgement of this, and a desperate attempt to overcome it, is the sliding scale method of commissions, where the rate rises after a certain level of sales has been reached. The sliding scale is only partially successful. The Complacency Plateau exists and nothing can eradicate it. The good manager can sometimes raise it for his men, he can encourage them to raise their sights, but this is something to talk about in chapter 7 on motivation.

As for exactly how much to pay a salesman in actual dollars, pounds, pesetas, zlotys, or cowrie shells—that is an impossible question to answer. Not only do pay scales vary from industry to industry, but most companies even have a different scale for the salesman working downtown Manhattan from the one whose territory is Spotted Horse, Wyoming.

Aside from utilizing figures published in your country's department of labor or industry bulletins, there are two methods for determining salary scales. The first is to throw up your hands and call in the consultants. There are highly specialized organizations using highly sophisticated methods who will feed your innermost secrets into computers and tell you what to pay your people. Many companies have more or less given the whole headache of pay scales over to these specialists and it seems to work for them. This method costs you, of course.

The other way is free and it should be more popular and widespread than it is. It is simply to form a coterie of personnel managers—say, ten to twelve—from companies in industries *similar* to your own to meet two or three times a year to compare salaries paid for similar jobs. This is not (or it should not be) a salary-fixing ring with the object of keeping pay scales down. It is an honest endeavour to discover what the job is worth on the open market and to make sure that you are keeping up with other companies in similar situations. I say "in *similar* situations." It is probably not a good idea to get as cosy as this with your direct opposition.

HOW TO PAY?

So much for how much to pay salesmen. Now for *how* to pay them. There are only five ways to pay salesmen, and here they are:

A. All salary. Here there is no commission whatever. Rain or shine, whether he brings in an empty order book or sells up a storm, he gets the same size check. The soap-and-toothpaste boys, oil company reps, and ethical drug salesmen usually get paid this way.

B. Mostly salary with small "incentive" commission. This is an attempt to add a cherry to the top of the cake. The salesman gets a living salary. It has to be a living salary because the commission is relatively small. The commission is often called an "incentive bonus," but there isn't much bonus and therefore not much incentive. Many industrial salesmen, as well as the furniture, soft goods, and allied trades, are paid like this.

C. Half salary, half commission. Here the remuneration is so arranged that the salesman takes home about half in fixed salary and half as a commission on sales—more if he has had a good month, less if things have been tight. Oddly enough, this is not a very popular way of payment. Most companies veer towards an emphasis on either salary or commission; they don't sit on the fence.

D. Mostly commission with small "retainer" salary. Here the salary part of his monthly check is much too small to live on and, in fact, it is hardly worthy of the name. It is more a sort of retainer, with the bulk of his income coming from sales volume. Automobile, typewriter, and similar salesmen are paid like this.

E. All commission. If the pure commission salesman doesn't sell he doesn't eat. If he sells well he can be sitting on a pile of diamonds with Elizabeth Taylor's younger sister in his lap. Often, these men are not strictly *employed* by their companies at all. Rather, they are under a contract as agents and are to all intents and purposes in business for themselves with, as it were, a franchise to sell the products of their principal. Speciality salesmen, life insurance agents, encyclopaedia men—these are the straight commission boys.

YOU GET WHAT YOU PAY FOR

Those are the five ways to pay salesmen, and the next question is: why? Why are different salesmen paid in different ways? Is there not a "best" way to pay them? The answer to that is the point of this chapter—*you get what you pay for,* not depending on how much you pay, but simply on *how* you pay. The truth is that you attract to your company a very different type of selling animal when you offer payment by all salary than you do by offering payment by all commission. Let us take these two extremes, the straight salary and the straight commission, and see what we can expect from each of them:

The salary salesman	*The commission salesman*
More order taking	More aggressive selling
A team man	A lone wolf
Company oriented	Sales oriented
Accepts supervision	Rejects supervision
Welcomes field training	Hates field training

Ambitious to climb the executive ladder	A "career" salesman doesn't want promotion
Steady rather than top producer	High producer, but sometimes erratic
Quality of selling usually good	Quality selling can be sacrificed for high volume

This comparison gives only a broad picture, and we all know salaried men with high sales volume and commission men who work well on a team, but it does usually work out something like this.

So, you get what you pay for. Does your marketing strategy need careful territory coverage, regular and meticulous paperwork, full credit information, repeat and repeat and repeat calling? Then you pay all or nearly all salary because you can't afford to have a commission-salesman personality within a thousand miles of your customers. Or do you need tough, aggressive selling, men who will go out calling at all hours, "one-shot" rather than repetitive selling, minimum supervision and, above all, high sales volume with the lowest cost to you? Then you pay straight commission or close to it because with the salary-salesman types you would slowly starve to death.

Some examples are in order to show just what I mean when I say that you get what you pay for. One company which sold office machines was paying its salesmen a decent salary with a small "incentive" commission (B). Its sales were somewhat disappointing, and when a new sales director was appointed he reckoned that he knew why: office equipment salesmen should never be paid a living salary. He had a meeting and his first words were; "I have asked you to come here today to tell you that your salaries are being cut by 75 percent." I suppose you could say that he immediately had the group's undivided attention. He then explained that the new commission system was so arranged that all each salesman had to do was sell exactly what he had been selling, and he would actually earn more. Of course, if he sold more than before he would be earning significantly more.

That was in February. By October of that year he had lost almost three-quarters of his original crew. He hadn't fired them, they had simply pulled out. He had hired more to replace them and had virtually a new team. This new team was a bunch of rebels who never attended sales meetings if it didn't suit their plans, who hated field supervision, who sent in call reports erratically or not at all, who would disappear for days at a time—and who sold as though the world was being switched off at midnight.

Could you stand this—not only on a short-term basis, but for the long haul? If you could, then pay straight commission or nearly so (*D* or *E*), and, probably, spend a good deal of your office time living on a diet of aspirin and fingernails. A highly successful manager of commission salesmen once told me; "I don't have much trouble with selection of salesmen. I hire the man I think is the best and I tell him that if he is not earning more than I am in three months he is going to be fired." So simple—if you can live with it.

One of my clients is in the business of supplying products to the automotive industry. They pay straight salary (*A*), and they asked me whether their sales would not increase if they changed to half salary, half commission (*C*) or even to mostly commission (*D*). I said that I was sure that sales would go up, and their eyes gleamed. I also said that they would, by changing, open up a Pandora's box of troubles which would make their heads swim, and I enumerated a few. I asked them whether they could live with all that. They thought about it and decided to stay with *A*.

What are the problems of handling commission salesmen? Here are a few, in no particular order:

He oversells with little regard to the true need or capacity of the customer, so that stock can deteriorate or become obsolete before it is used.

He does a bad job of territory coverage, calling only on those customers where immediate business is likely. This "Skimming the cream" off a territory can produce high volume for a time, but neglect of small or prospective customers is poor long-term marketing.

A high rate of return of stock, cancelations of orders, and demands for credit are likely to come from his territory.

His relations with his customers can often be strained, and the customers commonly complain to his office or even bar their doors to him.

His economy of operation is often poor—he will drive 4,000 miles in a month where 2,500 would cover the territory adequately.

Having sucked the easy part of his territory dry, he sometimes demands more area, or a new slot altogether.

Grim picture? But this is the commission salesman, warts and all, and many industries would fail completely if they did not have him.

Having been properly rude about the *E* man, are there any disadvantages connected with the straight *A* salesman? Indeed there are:

He tends to expect a good deal from his management in the way of help in selling—more even than good management is equipped to supply.

He often gets into a comfortable rut in his selling job, the "If it's Tuesday, this must be the northern suburbs" feeling.

He wants up the ladder too soon; you hired him as a salesman but he sees himself as a manager overnight.

He lacks the divine fire of a man who knows that income is totally and utterly dependent on whether or not he sells.

So, you pays your money and you takes your choice. You get what you pay for, both how much and also how you pay. It often seems to me that many of the problems of handling a group of salesmen stem from the fact that the company's remuneration scheme is completely wrong for the industry, and they have therefore attracted a completely wrong group of salesmen. Look well, therefore, at your own system; many of your headaches could start right there.

There is a faint wind of change in the concept of sales staff remuneration. In spite of the attendant problems, I notice a definite tendency to move away from all salary to some sort of commission payment, no matter how small it may be. This is so even in such unlikely industries as pharmaceuticals, where the salesmen rarely take an order at all but merely detail their products to doctors so that they will be prescribed for patients. I like the idea of some commission or other, and so long as we recognize the possible problems and don't go mad and rush right from straight salary to straight commission, the results will probably be worth while.

None of what we have discussed in this chapter has anything to to with incentive schemes and contests. These do not properly come under the heading of remuneration, and they are so important that they deserve a chapter to themselves. They get it (Chapter 10).

4

The Necessary Art
of Hiring

If you are a working sales manager you will not question the validity
of the title of this chapter. Sales staff selection is indeed a necessary
art. We can do a lot of things wrong in the management of
salesmen, but this is one thing we simply *must* get right. One
mistake in selection, one bad apple, can affect not only his own
territory, but also the others in your area.

Bad selection is also the one mistake which is very difficult to hide
from your superiors, since a salesman's performance is much easier
to judge than an office worker's. You can hide that lemon in the
personnel department by putting his desk behind the water cooler
and limiting his duties to nothing more esoteric than collecting the
coffee money, but a salesman is his territory, and substandard
performance shows up in the sales figures like a belly dancer in a
nunnery.

So we have a double problem, namely that one of the most
important aspects of a sales manager's job, the one which can have
the most disastrous consequences if it is not skillfully done, is also
that one in which we have little skill, natural aptitude, or formal
training. Let us accept that we are not naturally good selectors of
staff. If you find this offensive, then look at it this way: suppose I
took you to another company and allowed you to interview ten of
their salesmen. What would you give for your chances of picking
the best five out of the ten? How would you feel if your own job
depended on it? (It does depend on it, in a way.) I wouldn't bet more
than fifty cents on my chances of doing it, and I have been hiring,

training, and managing salesmen for most of my business life.

No, staff selection is not a natural skill, but it is so important that if it is properly done it can make up for lack of skill in many other aspects of management. It's true—pick your men really well and you do not need to have as much skill in motivation, control, organization, or employee appraisal.

I hate to admit this, but the hiring of salesmen is more important than the training of salesmen. There, I've said it. What makes it stick in my throat is that I am not a personnel expert, I am a trainer, and most of my business life has been a running battle with personnel people. But it is true that in producing a good sales team, their job is more important than mine.

Let us examine that statement. If you want a good team of salesmen then you hire good men and you train them to be better, right? And it makes much more sense to hire good men in the first place than to hire a bunch of clowns and then try to train them to be good salesmen, because it can't be done. Not even the best sales trainer in the world can turn a loser into a winner. I haven't in all my years as a trainer—and neither has anyone else. I recently saw an advertisement for a sales training course which invited companies to send their *worst* salesmen to the course. This outfit claimed a 92 percent success rate. All I can say is that if that were true, then I should be the first man to attend the course, because I would love to have the secret of turning bums into salesmen.

One of the silliest mistakes we make in sales staff selection is so obvious it is hardly worthwhile writing down, but we keep on making it. It is this: Suppose we are the managers of a company making and selling plumbing supplies, and we need a salesman. Now ideally we would like a man who is skilled in the plumbing trade who is also a top-level salesman. We will probably have trouble finding anyone with both of these worthy attributes, so we have to pick one of them, and as sure as nuts we pick the wrong one. Instead of hiring a good salesman and teaching him about plumbing supplies we hire a plumber and try to turn him into a saleman.

I am not knocking plumbers—some of my best friends are friends of plumbers. Nor am I saying that no plumber can ever be a good salesman. I am simply making the point that it is a lot easier to turn a salesman into an expert on a certain product than it is to turn the product expert into a salesman. If I seem to be getting a trifle hysterical on this point it is because having hired the plumber you then send him to a Michael Beer Sales Clinic and expect me to turn him into a crackerjack salesman. When I don't accomplish this miracle (which would be on a par with dividing the loaves and fishes) you say, "Well, Michael Beer's much-vaunted clinics boobed on this one." Maybe, but even it you sent him to a *good* sales course you would be asking the impossible.

This seems a good place to bring up the age-old question of whether a salesman is born or made. Now, every book on selling, every film, every sales course will tell you that the born salesman doesn't exist and that salesmen are made, through good training, management, counseling and supervision. I seem to be a lone voice in the wilderness on this point because I really believe that to a certain extent a salesman *is* born and not "made."

Sales trainers normally agree that salesmen are made, because the clear implication is that if you send your men to their training courses they will make them into salesmen. But it isn't true. It isn't true because a good salesman brings to the job certain basic characteristics, and if he does not have these characteristics he will *never* be a good salesman. Indeed he should never enter the selling business at all, because no amount of training will ever give him those characteristics. From that point of view, then, a salesman is born. Sure, training can take the rough casting and polish it until the final figure emerges, but if the casting is the wrong shape to start with, forget it.

On the other hand, another of the silliest cliches in selling is the oft-heard phrase, "A good salesman can sell anything." Rubbish. We all know excellent salesmen in, say, the fast-moving consumer field who would be fish out of water in capital goods selling. The whole approach to these two types of selling is so different, the skills and responsibilities expected of each so wide apart, that unless we have a job description, we could hire a man who has not the least chance of success.

THE JOB DESCRIPTION

A complete, carefully thought-out job description is essential to successful hiring. Some sales managers raise their eyebrows at the idea of a full, written job description for a salesman. Surely a salesman's job is simply to go out and move product? How much of a description does that take? Are we not merely adding to the pile of unnecessary paperwork which plagues the sales division? This attitude is a gross oversimplification. The salesman's job is not merely to "get out there and sell," and here is proof if you need it. Take just one little aspect of a salesman's job, that relating to competitive activity. You certainly want to know what the competition is doing in the field, don't you? Well, who better to tell you than the man in the front line, the salesman? Right, then. It goes down in his job description.

An excuse I hear in many management clinics for not using job descriptions is that the salesman will wave it in the manager's face when told to perform a certain task and demand to be shown where it says that he should do it. More rubbish. The job description can be written in such a way that it covers every single thing you could ever want him to do. I was not going to produce a job description in this book since, as I have said, these vary from industry to industry and company to company, but writing about it has psyched me up to where I jolly well am. Here it is:

JOB SPECIFICATION—SALESMAN

Responsible to: District Manager (line authority)
                    Product Manager (product matters)

BASIC FUNCTIONS

To promote profitable sales of product in his territory, ~~either directly or through retailers~~, in accordance with company policies and procedures.
To project a proper image of himself and of the company at all times.

OBJECTIVES AND RESPONSIBILITIES

To promote new business through an organized and ongoing prospecting system.
To maintain and increase present business by calling on and servicing present customers; to sell across the entire range; to trade up wherever possible.
To produce a regular planning list which covers his territory effectively and economically.
To render full and informative call reports to his District Manager at the intervals required of him.

To maintain an up-to-date and comprehensive customer record system.

To keep himself informed of, and report immediately, any significant competitive activity in his territory.

To open, with the approval of his District Manager, new dealerships in his territory.

To fill in credit application forms for new customers, and to satisfy himself, with the help of the Credit Department, of the credit standing of customers before committing himself to orders.

To collect overdue monies from customers where necessary.

To care for company transport entrusted to him and to ensure that it is in a clean and roadworthy condition.

To attend such sales meetings as are required, whether these are during or outside normal working hours.

To ensure that his sales literature, samples, sales aids, and demonstration kits are in good appearance and condition.

To suggest to his District Manager changes in his calling pattern, paperwork, or territory that would make his selling efforts more effective or economical.

To merchandise his products in retail outlets through effective use of display; to work with the company or dealer merchandisers in this regard.

To rotate stock in retail outlets to avoid old, shop-soiled, or dated stock.

To keep an up-to-date list of plant and equipment used by his customers.

To regrade his customers regularly on the basis of future expansion, potential, or penetration and to decide from this on the most effective call frequency for each customer; also, with the approval of his District Manager, to delete from his list such calls as are unprofitable now or will be in the future.

To report immediately and, within his authority limits, to act on, all customer complaints, and to ensure that these are dealt with to the mutual satisfaction of both customer and company.

To ensure that customers are fully acquainted with all products sold to them and, where necessary, to train customers' staff in the correct usage of these products.

To ensure, by reading trade journals, by attending outside courses and lectures, and through discussions both in and outside the company, that he is keeping up-to-date with developments in his industry.

To approach all situations with the company's point of view and welfare in mind.

That may not be a model for all job descriptions now or in the future, but there is not one word of padding in the whole thing; every single point is necessary for one salesman or another. Work from something like this and both you and your personnel manager will know what you're looking for.

ATTRACTING APPLICANTS

Before we can begin hiring salesmen we have to have some salesmen to hire, so we need to examine some ways to attract people (lure them, if you like) to apply for a job with us. There are three ways to do this: newspaper advertising, word of mouth, and piracy.

NEWSPAPER ADVERTISING

Newspaper advertising is still the most widely used method of attracting applicants for a sales job, even though many companies have discarded it in disgust after spending literally thousands on it with no worthwhile result. Still, an advertisement is the simplest way to let people know that you are in the market for salesmen.

Although I am no expert on advertising, there are a few basic points to observe when advertising for staff. First, be honest. Setting aside the question of ethics, you will save yourself a lot of time and irritation by being completely honest in your advertisement. The job you offer is door-to-door, cold-canvass selling? Say so. What in the world and hereafter do you gain by saying that you want "management trainees"? Do you actually enjoy plowing your way through thousands of letters and interviews which lead to nothing as soon as the applicant learns the truth?

Let's suppose that you want a salesman to sell a speciality line direct to housewives, on a straight commission basis. Recognize first that he is a special breed of animal. Nineteen out of twenty salesmen would not be caught dead in that sort of job and would in any case starve to death if they took it on. That sort of commissioned, door-to-door selling, although it has become a sort of joke (the vacuum-cleaner salesman is as corny a chestnut as mothersin-law and lodgers), is nevertheless the purest form there is. That man is a *salesman,* and you can believe it. You are therefore looking for the one man in twenty who likes knocking on doors and who can make a living at it. Why not look for him like this?

Commission Salesman

We are looking for a salesman who wants to make money. He will have to find his own prospects and make his own sales. Our product is a necessity in every home. Its quality is superior and its price is competitive. We will back him with good parts and service facilities, but he will be in business for himself. We offer no company car, no salary, no field supervision—merely the chance to make more money than most executives do. Our commission terms are very generous, and we will train you to find the customers and sell to them. If you have the drive to run yourself as a business, sponsored by a fast-growing, international organization, then write to the sales manager, ABC company, for a chance to learn more.

This may not be the finest advertisement for salesmen ever written, but it is completely honest, and the man who answers it can be under no illusions as to exactly what he is letting himself in for.

When you have written an advertisement, can you honestly say that you can back every word in it? For instance, most companies almost automatically put in something like "Excellent prospects for advancement." It seems to be a sort of talisman that they stick in. If you have put it in your advertisement, can you support it if you are seriously challenged? I have seen this bit of fiction in advertisements when the truth is that the companies are already top heavy with people, all of whom are expecting imminent promotion. "But we promote on merit, not on length of service!" you say, innocently astonished. I know you do, but come *on,* for heaven's sake. Excellent prospects? Pull the other one, it's got bells on it. If a man does join you, how long will it take him to discover the true position? How will he feel about you when he does? How long will he stay after that? Whose fault will it be when he leaves?

Be honest. It is indeed the best policy, long term.

The second pointer: Don't hide the company name. I am never impressed by advertisements which ask the applicant to write to "Box 1234," and I don't think that salesmen are, either. The usual excuse for not stating the company name in staff appointment advertisements is: "We don't want our opposition to know what we are doing." So? All you are admitting is that you want more salesmen, and what is so secret about that? And don't kid yourself—your opposition probably knew before you did that you needed more people.

The point is that if you don't say who you are, you may scare off a lot of potentially good applicants who are saying, "I'd like to answer that, but what if it's my own company?" Anyway, there is something a little sneaky about an anonymous advertisement. You expect him to give you his name but you are hiding yours. Why? Are you ashamed of it?

Third, be informative. Tell as much as you can about the precise nature of the job. You needn't give a full job description in an advertisement, but try to pin down what *sort* of salesman you want. Something like this, for instance:

> *Salesman wanted, to sell our line of high-quality automotive tools. Our customers are the bigger hardware stores and service stations. The territory is semi-rural and will take the salesman away from home for five days in a month. Experience in our line is not essential, but it would suit a man who is interested in the automotive field.*

Putting that paragraph in the advertisement will help to ensure that you don't get an application from a salesman of French underwear who hates leaving home.

Fourth, tell him the price. I accept arguments against this point, and I concede that there are times when it may not be advisable. Generally, though, it is a good idea to put at least a salary range down. If you are worrying about your competition again and thinking that you are giving away company secrets, stop worrying. They already have a fairly good idea of what you pay your men, just as you have about them. Besides, putting in a salary range has two advantages: it will chase away the applicants who are looking for far more than you pay and who will only waste your time, and it may attract some good men who had no idea that the job carried such a good tag.

If you work on the Scrooge syndrome, then of course you will not mention the salary at all, and when the time comes for discussing the price you will haggle him down to the very least that he will take. Whereupon he will join your company knowing that you are a small-minded skinflint and the work you get from him will be in direct proportion to what you pay him. You will deserve each other.

Fairly obviously, the best medium for advertising is the daily press. Salesmen don't read trade and financial papers, although these may be all right if you want to hire managers. Evening or Sunday papers are better than morning papers. Would you want to hire a salesman who has time to read a paper in the morning? (Later in this chapter we shall examine a most effective way to use Sunday papers to attract good applicants.)

Word-of-Mouth

Many companies use word-of-mouth to find salesmen. In fact, I have clients who use no other. Here you simply tell your present staff that you need more people, using the bulletin board, the house magazine, a memo to each salesman, or an announcement at the next sales meeting, and you ask your people to tell their friends about the job. Some companies even offer a small bonus to the man who introduces a successful applicant, so long as he stays with the company for six months.

The advantages of this method are manifold. First, it is cheap. Second and far more important, the man who applies has, you may be sure, had a long and intimate chat with his sponsor, and before ever he steps into your office for the interview he has a very good idea of exactly what the job entails, which means that he is far less likely to waste your time by being an impossible bet. Third, there is a certain degree of automatic qualifying for the job, since your present man is hardly likely to recommend a dud because that won't help his own image in the company. (There is another way of looking at this, and that is that if I recommend a really good man, then he and I could later both be bucking for the same promotion—and the man I set up might get the job instead of me! Luckily, few salesmen seem to think this way.)

Naturally, the word-of-mouth system works only if the morale of your present people is high. If not, the attitude will be: "I'm stuck here until I can find a better deal, but there's no way that I am going to inflict my buddy with a job in this place!"

PIRACY

The name you put to the third method of attracting staff depends on who is doing it to whom. If other companies are doing it to you, you call it "piracy"; if you are doing it to others the term is "intra-industry selection." Call it what you prefer, it is the practice of seducing people away from other companies in your own industry, usually by personal contact. Most of my clients either use it themselves or suffer from it, losing their own men to their competitors.

I am against the practice, but not from ethical considerations because there is surely nothing unethical in it. My reluctance to use it stems from experience: few salesmen hired in this way ever seem to turn out quite as good as expected. Perhaps it is because the emphasis in the approach is wrong. If you approach a man and say, "We have heard about you and we would like very much to talk to you about joining us," that salesman, if he is human, is going to say to his wife, "Hey, these people *need* me! Watch me dictate the conditions of the deal." In this case you are the applicant, not him, and the whole atmosphere of the discussion is distorted.

Also, never forget one thing: if a man comes to your company for the only reason that you are paying him more than his previous employers, then you have not bought him, you have only rented him for a while, and *he is still in the market.* Another 10 percent offer and he has vanished like a jellybean in a kindergarten, and your intra-industry selected man has been pirated by that unethical mob across the road.

PERSONNEL AGENCIES

Actually there's a fourth method of attracting applicants. If you like heated arguments, then bring up the subject of personnel consultants in any group of managers. There will appear two widely differing schools of thought. On the one hand there will be the managers who use an outside agency and who have had consistently good results from their recommendations, and on the other there will be the people who have spent hundreds or thousands with agencies and who have hired a lot of dropouts and wasters.

Personnel agencies are rather like the girl with the curl in the middle of her forehead—when she was good she was very, very good, and when she was bad she was horrid. If you decide to try this method then choose your agency carefully. It is not intrusive to ask for references from other clients of theirs (not your opposition) and to check up on them.

It is a prime rule when working with these people *never to hide anything from them*. Tell them everything they want to know, or don't expect them to do a good job for you. Indeed, any agency worth its salt will refuse to act for you unless you are completely frank with them.

There are two ways in which to use an agency. One way is for you to do the advertising, the interviewing, and checking on references, and then, having got down to a short list, to send these last few hopefuls to the agency. There they will undergo a series of tests and interviews designed to discover everything about them from manual dexterity and performance under stress through how they coped with the trauma induced by the death of the family cat when they were seven years old. (I'm not sneering. Who knows how important this might be?) The agency thereupon sends you a confidential report on each applicant.

The other way is where the agency does all the advertising and preliminary work and sends you the short list people with their recommendations. This last way is much more expensive than the first because the agency is doing much more, and the usual scale of fees is between 10 and 15 percent of the man's first year's salary. Don't let this scare you, because if you get a good man it is cheap at twice the price.

A final word: the personnel agency can't make your decision for you, and no good agency ever will. All they can say is; "Here is Waldo. We like him because of so-and-so, in spite of so-and-so. We think he merits consideration." You walk the last mile on your own.

SUNDAY ON THE PHONE

I promised to give details of an effective way to use the Sunday papers to attract applicants. It isn't my idea and I have no notion of where it came from, but it works. It is unpopular with sales managers because it completely wrecks a Sunday, but you have been pulling down that big salary all this time and who said your job was easy?

Here it is: An advertisement is placed in the Sunday papers, or Saturday night will serve even better sometimes. It should be prominently displayed, *not* buried in the "Help Wanted" columns. It tells all about the job (as much as possible in an advertisement) and then very clearly it says something like this:

> Don't *write to us. We respect your wish for anonymity. You don't want us to know your name until you know much more about us and about the job. Instead of writing, pick up your telephone now and I will answer your call. My name is Cyril Filstripp and I am the sales manager of Vertical Cuboids Co. Here is my number. I promise I won't ask for your name or for any details which will identify you until you* want *to tell me. Instead, I'll tell you more about the job. If you are still interested, then maybe we can get together for a confidential interview. I shall be at my telephone only between 9 and 5 today (Sunday). Please don't call at any other time. If you fit the qualifications described above and if you would like to move to a dynamic, international outfit where merit is rewarded, then call me. It could change your life for the better.*

It really does wreck the Sunday because you are stuck at the telephone for the entire period mentioned in the advertisement. Be careful to qualify the job as much as you can so that you get as few "impossibles" as possible. Be prepared to give your sales talk many times, and prepare in advance for every question which inquirers are likely to throw at you. You are ready with questions of your own, of course, and these are intended to find out if the caller is suitable, but the questions must honor your promise not to identify the caller until he is ready to tell you his name. If it seems to both of you that it is worth getting together, then at last you have to have his name, but not until then.

This method works. I have proved it myself and I know several companies who have used it with great success. Why does it work? Well, who do you want applying to you for a job? Do you want a man who is unemployed, or do you want a man who already has a good job? This is the man who in the ordinary way would not dream of *writing* to apply for a job. He fears that it may somehow get back to his present employers that he is looking (it often does, no matter how many assurances of strict confidence are given), and he doesn't dare to jeopardize his position. He is attracted by the idea of the anonymity: *you will not ask him for his name*. "What the hell," he says to himself, "what have I got to lose?" And he picks up the telephone.

This method is a nuisance, but it works. Use it and you will get a much higher standard of applicant than with any other.

SCREENING THE APPLICANTS

Very well, we can now assume that we have progressed to the stage where people have actually applied to us for interviews. Now comes the sorting-out process, the business of selection. A typical selection process could look like the following. In fact, these figures are taken from an industrial client of mine which usually hires four or five new salesmen at a time. The company has a good public image and an advertisement can result in about eighty applications. These go first to the personnel manager, *not* to the sales division. It is not the job of anyone in sales to fight his way through eighty letters. That's what your company has a personnel man for, so let him do it.

The personnel manager has grown old and cynical in the business and is therefore not impressed with the pile of letters on his desk. He knows too well that of the eighty at least fifty are "floaters." This is a man who drifts from job to job seeking the dream job (which he has yet to realize does not exist). Let's spend a minute with the floater before we forget him forever. The biggest moment of his day is when he sits down with the evening paper and a red pencil and goes through the jobs offered, marking those which look more attractive than the one he has now. He writes several letters of application every week of his life and has several interviews every month.

I think that sales managers would rise straight up out of their chairs in a sitting position if they realized how many floaters there are around. Are there ten or more men in your sales team? Then you have at least one floater and probably more, and the best thing you can do is find him and consign him to the outer darkness, because he isn't *working* for you, he is merely "associated with the company," while he uses your time and petrol traveling between interviews for a better job. The heck with him.

So. The personnel manager recognizes the floaters for what they are (most of them, anyway, since he is not infallible), and they get a standard letter thanking them and saying that while their qualifications are impressive, nevertheless blah blah blah. He scrutinizes the remaining thirty and decides to send them a letter, probably enclosing an application form, since this is better than having them fill in the form when they come for an interview. Filling in the form at the interview is not only time-wasting in itself, but very often something in the form knocks the applicant out of further consideration and you have wasted his time and yours by asking him to appear.

The personnel manager gets about twenty of the forms back duly filled in (the other ten have fallen by the wayside) and he sorts these into rejects and "worth interviewing." He interviews, say, fifteen and discards half of them. At this stage, probably heartily sick and tired of the whole affair, he hands the rest to the sales manager and washes his hands of the problem. Whereupon the sales manager selects his four with all the calm, assured skill of a cow on a skateboard. An uncharitable comparison, perhaps, but so many mistakes are made in staff selection that one wonders if it wouldn't be better to close one's eyes and use the pinsticking method. The results in many cases couldn't be worse.

SOME SELECTION PRINCIPLES

Here are some points to consider when hiring staff, especially sales staff. They are broad and general, and you will have to adapt them to your own specific selection problem.

1. Know exactly what you want. So often we don't *get* exactly what we want in a salesman because we don't *know* exactly what we want. Here I am making another impassioned plea for a carefully written job description, produced for that specific job, and put down on paper before we even advertise. The title "salesman" can mean very different things in different companies, and an expert salesman in one field can be a miserable failure in another. Spare yourself the burden of having a miserable salesman in your employ by knowing in detail what you want in your man—*and by telling your applicant what you want.*

I began to save myself a lot of time and irritation when I used a written job description in the actual interview. Before we even started talking I would hand it to the applicant and say, "This is what we expect a salesman for this company to be and to do. Perhaps you would like to read it before we talk." In several cases, he put down the sheet after going through it, rose, and said, "Sorry—I didn't realize that it was that sort of job. It doesn't sound like my sort of thing at all." Do this and save yourself time and money—and grief. Try this if you haven't done so already, and you will find that it is a fine way to get into the interview. You will know exactly what you want—and so will the applicant.

2. *Hire well ahead.* Many bad salesmen have been hired because the manager is caught behind the eight ball. "We must have a man by Monday—anybody!" And that is what we generally find ourselves with—anybody. Any hiring policy worthy of the name is geared to future needs, and people are hired well in advance of those needs. Thus we can sort out the misfits and train and develop the promising boys well ahead of the time when we actually send them out into their own territories.

There is the objection that having trainee salesmen cluttering up the place, eating off you without producing, is an expensive exercise, and in a way this is true. However, they are not merely sitting around bending paperclips and chatting up the typists. You have arranged a formal working program for them and they are busy with this on a fulltime basis. Not, mind you, a sort of "Sit next to Joe and see what he does and then watch Charlie for a while" affair, where they are merely breathing down the necks of the regular workers and being bored to death. No, they are actually working in each department, and every phase of the program is slowly fitting them better for the job of salesman.

There are companies who never hire salesmen at all, only sales trainees, and these men are clearly told: "You will be working in the office for anywhere from six to eighteen months. If you develop satisfactorily, you will be *promoted* to the job of salesman." Great idea, for two reasons. First, I like the idea of a man being promoted to salesman because this way he realizes the importance of the job. Second, a salesman is a better man and a lot more useful if he has spent a few months at the order desk. He has been working with the intricacies of pricing and deliveries and has the experience to know what can be expected of the internal staff and what is absolutely impossible.

3. *Check, check, check every reference.* If there is a key point in this section it is right here. Checking references is bothersome and time consuming, but it is vital if we are not to be badly stung. The problem is that people don't write the truth in references. I don't, you don't, and the man who wrote the reference which is lying on your desk now didn't. You have "released" one of your men because he isn't up to the job. (You are too humanitarian, or too chicken, to fire him, so you "release" him, which merely means that you allow him to tell other companies that he left of his own accord.) He has the nerve to ask you for a reference, and you give him one. The truth is that he is shiftless, incompetent, and not very intelligent, but you gloss over these in the reference and stress his honesty, his good relations with customers, and the neat way he fills in paperwork. Which is all very fine, and it leaves you with a clear conscience and a nice warm feeling, but what about the unfortunate manager who, on the basis of your reference, then hires that guy you "released"? He ends up with the same lemon which you had finally gotten off your back.

People don't *write* the truth, but they are often willing to *tell* the truth, and a check on the telephone (or, if you are willing to spend the time, a personal visit) is worth it every time. This is not difficult. Having introduced yourself and said that you would like to confirm some points about their ex-employee (your applicant), you might ask some questions such as these: Exactly when did he leave the company? Why? What were his strong points? What were his weak points? How did he get on with people? What was his salary? That sort of thing. Finally, the most useful question of all: Would you consider rehiring him?

What usually happens here is that you are told, "We have a policy of never rehiring." You have to bypass this by saying that you realize that, but if there was no such policy, would they consider rehiring him? I have asked this question many times when checking references, and sometimes there is a short silence on the other end of the telephone and I hear, "Over my dead body!" Which, after all, is what you want to know. On the other hand you may be told, "Yes, I believe we would consider having him back. We were sorry to see him go, but he felt that his future was elsewhere and we didn't try to stand in his way. He's a sound man." Again, this tells you what you want to know.

A very real difficulty is that your applicant can't very well ask the company he now works for for a reference, and any other reference is probably out of date. Here the only course open to you if he seems to fit the bill is to hire him on the strict understanding that once he has resigned from his present company you will be checking with them, and the contract is valid only if nothing comes to light which differs significantly from the information he has given you. I enforced this once when, on checking, it appeared that far from working with the company, he had been fired two months before, and he had also boosted his salary by 20 percent. This man was most indignant when we canceled the job on him, accusing us of breaking our word because of a few trivial points. Tough, but so it goes.

4. *Avoid the "old school tie" effect.* You are across the desk from the applicant and are trying to find something in his record which will tell you whether he is the right man for the job or not. You notice in his application form that he went to the Diagonal High School in your home town. Well, what do you know! We were a great bunch of fellows at Diagonal! Before you know it you are chatting about the old days at D.H.S. and practically swapping pants with him. Of *course* you must hire him—why, he's our sort of people!

This problem is not confined to old school buddies, of course. We tend to like and have confidence in people who have the same sort of background we have, the same interests and hobbies, the same accent, and the same likes and dislikes—and we end up hiring a failure who looks just like us. This hiring in our own image is one of the mistakes most difficult to avoid in selection. We can easily acknowledge the danger, but we continue to do it. It is a very good argument for the "chain interview" method, where the applicant has several interviews with different people (one at a time, of course—we are not a group of army officers interviewing a candidate for officers' training school), who then get together and compare notes. This dilutes the "old school tie" problem, and it has the additional advantage of sharing the blame if he turns out to be a dud. ("What do you mean, my choice? I never liked him from the start—you were the one who wanted him!")

5. *Don't rely on appearance.* Appearance is important. You don't want a salesman carrying the business card of your company who looks as though he moonlights as a bouncer in a house of ill fame. The mistake we make here is to *rely* on his appearance, the way he talks and handles himself, and to hire on these. Do this and you will get a character I call "the professional job-getter," and you need him like a hangnail. He makes a vocation out of coming across well, and it is only after you have had him for six months that you realize that he has nothing behind the attractive facade. The manager who says, "I like him, he's sincere, he looks you right in the eye and he has a good, firm handshake," apparently fails to recognize that this man *practices* that open, honest look and that he-man handshake—it is part of his stock-in-trade.

6. *Don't oversell the job.* The stage is very easily set for this mistake. We like the man who is applying: "This fellow would be a real asset to the organization—we can't afford to lose the chance of getting him." So what do we do? We do a high-pressure selling job on him. We lean back, snap our suspenders, and sound off like a barker at a sideshow. We talk lyrically about the tremendous opportunities in the company. We give him some rags-to-riches case histories of men who have succeeded dramatically after being with us for only five minutes—we do everything except offer him a seat on the board. Highly flattered and impressed, he takes the job. When none of these wonderful things happen to him, he becomes disillusioned and quits and we have another expensive mistake to go against our record.

TRAFFIC LIGHTS METHOD

Finally, you might care to use a system of mine which I call "The Traffic Lights Method." A traffic light has three colors—red, yellow, and green, generally described as meaning "stop," "caution," and "go." I find it a simple matter to apply these to the applicant for a job, since every man has something in his background or record that makes us feel that we should stop any further idea of hiring him, that we should approach the idea with caution before we take further action, or that we should go ahead and take him on. We'll take the three "lights" one at a time.

THE RED LIGHTS

The "red lights" could be called "write-off" factors, because any single one of them will mean that we write the applicant off from any further consideration for employment *no matter how good he is otherwise*. Sometimes he is so suitable in some respects that we are blinded to these write-off factors. I saw a man hired to sell office equipment, which entailed lugging heavy machines from one office to another, in spite of the fact that he was badly crippled from polio and had difficulty in climbing a short flight of stairs unaided. For this particular job his disability was a write-off factor, no matter how good he was otherwise.

What are some other red lights? It often depends on the job, but here are a few: unwillingness to travel away from home, health problems, inability to absorb technical information about the products, age (where he has to fit into a company pension scheme), a history of alcoholism, and so on. You will have to make up your own set of red lights to fit your job requirements, but however you do it, have them clearly spelled out for yourself before you examine a man's suitability for hiring.

THE GREEN LIGHTS

The green lights are those things about the applicant which could make you feel that he is particularly suitable for the job. Again, they depend on the job itself, but a few sample green lights could be a special knowledge of the industry, in-depth product knowledge and application, excellent rapport with people, good attitude towards the job, good potential for promotion, specific qualifications, and so on. None of them enough to hire on alone, but all tending to make us think that he could indeed be the man.

Neither the red nor the green lights are too difficult to spot or to appreciate; they are mostly self-explanatory. It is the yellow lights which are the tough ones.

THE YELLOW LIGHTS

A yellow light is something in the applicant's background or record which, while it does not damn him, deserves deeper investigation. It is truly a "caution" matter. Is it so serious that it turns into a red light, or is there a perfectly innocuous explanation? Again it must be emphasized that there is no rigid list of yellow lights, that they vary with the job requirements. But here, as a guide only, are some yellow lights which I look for when evaluating applicants. You like them, you use them; you don't like them, make up your own list.

Itchy feet. This is not a skin condition, it merely indicates that the applicant has a record of moving from job to job rather quickly. The problem here is simply that if he has had four jobs in the last seven years, what makes you think that you can hold him? Is he a natural rambling rose? And if you believe him when he says, "Ah, but those other jobs were only to prepare me for this position with you—here is where I can find my true home," then you will have no difficulty in believing that pickles grow on trees.

Gaps in his job record. He left one company in July and joined the next one in November. Where was he? In jail? Now, this is a typical yellow light. There could well be the most innocent explanation, but you want that explanation, and it must gel.

Older but not better. Does his record show any advancement at all, or has he simply been getting older? Are there any signs of increased responsibility or greater sophistication in the job? (If you merely want a man to call on twelve outlets every day and take eight orders which have already been written out for him by the customer, then this is probably not a yellow light, but we are discussing *salesmen.*)

Domestic problems. And now we must ask ourselves just what business it is of ours what his personal life is like outside office hours. The answer is that it is no business of ours at all, *unless it interferes with the job,* and we all know that it can indeed interfere with his job performance. A man can be bigger or smaller in his job, depending on what is waiting for him at home. The attitude of the marriage partner can have a tremendous effect on the man's attitude, and domestic strife is a yellow light which we cannot ignore.

It takes a spot of moral courage to broach the subject with an applicant, but it must be done if there is the slightest sign of this yellow light in any of the checking we have done on him. Some companies make it a practice to see the wife of the applicant, perhaps in an informal setting. It isn't a bad idea to be able to talk to her, to tell her something about her husband's new job, get her reactions, and answer any questions she may have.

Money problems. Again, is it any business of ours? Yes, if it is going to interfere with his performance. He may be so busy dodging final demands for payment, repossessions, and garnishee orders that he doesn't have time to do much selling for us. You will never get this yellow light from him, of course, but it may well come out in the telephone checking you do on his references.

Too much brain for the job. Tricky one, this. Always beware of the PhD who wants to sell carbon paper because it is ten to one that he will get so bored with the job that he won't last. A similar question should arise with the man who is willing to accept a much lower salary than he has been used to. On this one, of course, we have to consider the economy of the day. This is being written at a time when good people are walking the streets, when a man can pick up his pay check at the end of the month and find that he simply doesn't have a job any more. He is under the whip, and it is nothing against the unfortunate man that he is prepared to lower his sights so that he can feed his family.

To many managers the fact that a man does not have a job is a yellow light in itself. All right, but tie that in with the times we live in, where mergers, takeovers, and companies folding up and dying are the order of the day. This could be the best time to get a good man, and forget the fact that he is jobless, but if you adopt the Scrooge principle and pay him slave wages simply because he is desperate for a job, then you deserve to lose him the moment times get better.

He has been his own boss. If he has a history of self-employment, if he has worked as his own boss, then the pattern is that he will eventually go back to working for himself, because (and I should know) working for yourself is such good fun that it is hard to get back into harness again. He may be applying for a job simply as a steppingstone between bankruptcies. It is a yellow light and only a very frank talk with him may switch the light off in your mind.

He bad-mouths his old boss. For me, any indication of ill-feeling about the last job or employer is a very strong yellow light. When he tells you that he left the company because "they were a bunch of crooks" then you have real cause to worry. In nine cases out of ten there was indeed some hanky-panky there, but it was on his side and not on the company's. Even if investigation shows that his old employers were somehow to blame, I don't like it. Surely he should be perceptive enough to realize that sounding off like that doesn't create a good impression. A personal prejudice, perhaps, but a yellow light nevertheless.

A yellow light is something which we need to investigate further, and we do not cross it off until the investigation has shown that it is of no significance. Make up your own list, have it in the forefront of your mind, and ignore it at your peril.

A FINAL WORD

A final thought on staff selection. I have left it to the last because if you learn only one thing from this chapter, then make it this. Failing to heed this is probably the biggest single reason that we hire bad people:

Don't hire the best of a bad bunch.

You have six men to consider for one sales job. Obviously, you have to reject five of them and, equally obviously, you go about it by eliminating the least suitable first. You say: "Well, Tom is the weakest of the whole lot, so cross him off. Then Horace is next weakest. Bye-bye Horace. Then, Archie . . ." and so on. This is the only way to do it, really, and you go on until you have one man left. So far, so good. But here is where we can make a terrible mistake: we automatically hire that last man. Why not? He is the best! But that is not the question. The question is not whether he is the best of the bunch, it is whether he measures up to the standards of the job, and we forget this, time and time again.

I recall attending a prize-giving at my daughters' school some years ago. One of the prizes was highly coveted, and speculation was intense as to who would be the lucky girl. The principal announced that the prize would not be awarded that year, and I heard some very unhappy parents complaining at the decision. It was an excellent decision, however. The principal was obviously too well bred to say it, but what she meant was: "No girl was good enough to deserve the prize, and we don't pick the best of a bad bunch!"

Neither should we.

5

The Endless Art of Training

The vanity of teaching doth oft make a man forget he is a blockhead.
THE MARQUIS OF HALIFAX, 1633-1695

You have hired a group of salesmen and it is now necessary to train them. In fact, of course, few managers are fortunate enough to start off with a team they have hired themselves. What almost invariably happens is that you are promoted into a job where there is already a sales force. These men are your legacy from the manager who occupied your chair before you, and they are now yours for better or for worse, in sickness and in health, until a better offer from another company do you part.

In large organizations there is a separate training division. In smaller companies training is simply another hat which the sales manager wears. In either case, the sales manager must be closely involved with the training and development of his men. You cannot under any circumstances whatever leave this aspect of manage-ment to the training people, believing that it is their job and why don't we simply let them get on with it. Just as you are involved in staff selection even though you have a personnel department, so you must be involved in training even though you have a training division.

Let us first distinguish between two completely different types of sales staff development—that of *teaching* and that of *training*. There certainly is a difference, although few managers realize it, and it is not merely a quibble. The following will do as working definitions: Teaching is the transmission from the teacher to the pupil of *knowledge;* training is the inculcation of *skills*.

Let us acknowledge right away that for practical purposes we tend to lump all staff development under the convenient heading of "Training," and there is nothing wrong with this. We shall be doing just that in this chapter. However, never forget that there is a difference and that we must break down the two concepts to see exactly what we are about.

KNOWING YOUR PRODUCT

Take teaching first. What sort of knowledge does a salesman need? First and perhaps most important is product knowledge, and don't skip this bit under the impression that you don't need it, because you very likely do. We do a lot of things wrong in the development of our salesmen, but nothing quite as bad as this—that we send them out into the marketplace without a proper knowledge of what it is that they are selling. Without having met your sales team, I will bet right now that fewer than one in five really knows his products, their application, their strong and weak points, and knows them backwards, and forwards, and sideways.

If I sound irritable about this business of product knowledge, it is because throughout my working year I walk into conference rooms to give groups of salesmen the skills of salesmanship, and I find that under a thin veneer of product knowledge *they do not know what they are selling*. Oh, they can tell you that it comes in four colors, that it cures athlete's foot and the King's evil, that it contains corrosive sublimate, that delivery time is four months and that it has a shelf life of three months, that you mustn't drink it if there is an R in the month, and that in Uganda they rub it into their hair to ensure a good yam crop.

Hell, that's not enough! Your men have got to *live* the product. They must know so much about what they sell that nobody can ever ask them a single question they can't answer—or know immediately where to find the answer. They must be so hungry for in-depth product knowledge that they are prepared to ride right over you in their never-ending quest for it. They must realize that they will *never* know enough about their products, that product training *never* stops—I am beginning to foam at the mouth, so enough, but that is telling it like it is.

I often give my groups a brief quiz to try to show them that they don't know enough about what they sell. Here are three typical types of selling with a few of the questions:

Automobile salesmen. What is Alec Issigonis famous for? (He invented the Mini, one of the most significant automotive designs of all time.) What is the function of the coil in an internal combustion engine? (It raises the voltage from 12 to about 18,000. That's all it does.)

Pharmaceutical salesmen. Where are the Islands of Langerhans? (In the human pancreas.) Banting and Best produced one of the most glorious failures in the history of medicine. What was it? (They failed to find a cure for diabetes, but in the process they discovered insulin.)

Oil salesmen. What is a stratigraphic trap? (It is a type of geological formation where oil is found.) What is a Christmas tree? (It is a cluster of control valves used to cap an oil well.)

I don't ask these questions to show how smart I am. Any fool can ask questions in one minute which a wise man can't answer in a year. I am merely making the point that the professional salesman *really* knows his product, and that means everything about it. *Everything.*

The point is sometimes raised that this in-depth product knowledge will turn the salesman into a sort of university lecturer when he talks to prospective customers. This would be the kiss of death, of course, but it doesn't have to happen. Product knowledge *by itself* may tend to produce the lecture type of sales talk, but this is where selling skills come in, and any sales training course worth the name will make it very clear that the customer does not buy the product merely because the taper roller bearings are ground to a tolerance of three microns. That fact will give the customer the reliability that he needs, and he buys reliability and not taper roller bearings. But until the salesman *knows* about the bearings he can't talk about the reliability.

It is also true that the salesman may never use half of the knowledge he has about his products, so why burden him with it? Simply because it is only when he does know that he can go out and talk with real confidence about the product, without worrying that someone is going to make him look stupid by asking a question he can't answer. That by itself is reason enough. He may indeed never use it, but ask him anything and he knows the answer. He *knows*.

And making sure he knows is nobody's job but yours.

KNOWING YOUR ENEMY

Almost equally important as product knowledge is a sound knowledge of *competitive* products. Your salesmen do not know how good their products are until they know how good their opposition is, and they cannot sell against that opposition until they have that knowledge. Right here is a plea from my heart: *please don't cheat your salesmen about the opposition.* If they have something in their product which is a strong selling point for them and which you don't have in your product, *then tell your salesmen!* Tell them fully, freely, and frankly, go into the opposition product in depth, take a whole sales meeting to do it, make sure they understand it—and you will give them confidence in you, in your company, and in your product.

This sounds contradictory, doesn't it? Tell them how good the opposition product is and it will make them more confident about their own product. How can that be? Yet it is so. Knowledge does not cause fear in a salesman's heart, ignorance causes fear—ignorance of just how good the opposition is. Without in-depth knowledge of the opposition, frightening questions fill his mind: What's their product like? How is it better than ours? Can we ever hope to sell against it?

Suppose you hide from him all knowledge of his enemy. He will find out about it, be very sure of that, and he will find it in the worst place possible, namely, right in front of a potential customer. He will walk in brimming with enthusiasm and zeal and start his sales presentation, and somewhere along the line the script will go something like this:

Salesman: And not only that, our machine is guaranteed for twelve months on parts and labor, and not only that—
Customer: Hold it, hold it. Where's your squiggle moderator?
Salesman: My—what?
Customer: Your squiggle moderator, son! Where's the gadget on

this machine of yours to moderate squiggles under conditions of high flux?

Salesman: Er, *squiggle* moderator. Er, duh.

Customer: You don't have one, do you?

Salesman [*feeling that there must be an easier way of making a living*]: Squiggle *moderator—*

Customer: Well, your competitor has one fitted to his machine, and I need it. We get a lot of high flux conditions around here and I can't afford an extreme squiggle situation. Sorry, friend—no sale. I'm buying the opposition. Whereupon your salesman gets falling-down drunk, resigns, and the next you hear from him he is an elevator operator in a single-story building and it is your fault.

This situation came about because of insufficient knowledge of the salesman's own product and complete ignorance of the opposition. On the face of it, a squiggle moderator sounds like a good thing to have. But if the opposition is forced to include one in their machines because of a basic design weakness, and if the brilliance of your design eliminates squiggles no matter how high the flux conditions are, then we have a very different scene, and your salesman has a right to know about it.

Even if the damn moderator is something you would like to have, *you must tell them about it.* Concede freely that the opposition is a good product, examine its good points—and then counter these with equally good points of your own. Being completely honest about this is the only way to ensure that your salesman hits the selling arena with complete confidence in his products and his manager—and that's you.

I once ran a sales clinic for a company and I was never asked to do another one for them. This is because I failed to conceal my shocked disbelief when the boss blandly informed me that he had instituted a cast-iron rule that the name of the opposition product never be mentioned in the offices of his company. Whether he had decided that if everybody closed their eyes and pretended that the opposition did not exist it would quietly disappear, I really don't know. I do know that this rule will immediately have a profound effect on a salesman. He will realize that his own boss is scared silly by the opposition! This sort of thing makes me wonder how some companies stay in business.

No military commander wants to go into battle without knowing what force is arrayed against him, what personnel strength, what guns, tanks and rockets he will meet. Neither should a salesman have to enter the arena without as much opposition knowledge as possible.

KNOWING YOUR CUSTOMER

The third aspect of knowledge I would like my team to be imbued with is actually the easiest part of selling: knowing your customer. Now, creative selling is hard. Creative selling is the process of making a sale where there was apparently no sale to be made, of changing a man's thinking from "I don't need any, thank you" to "Yes, please send me some." Changing it, not by high-pressure tactics or slick gimmicks, but through a logical and convincing presentation.

Creative selling is hard, and nowhere in my sales clinics is there anything to make it easy. It can be made *easier,* however, simply through knowing your customer. Customer knowledge is not difficult to gain. It is merely boring, uninspiring, and time-consuming, which are three excellent reasons for salesmen to duck it. *They must not duck it.* It is the biggest single reason that a sale is made where there was no apparent chance of making that sale. If this sounds too facile, then delve with some of your salesmen into the real reasons they lost the last three sales they expected to get and you will probably find that if they had known some fact about the customer, his business, his needs, his problems, and his hang-ups they may just have won through.

The longer I work with salesmen, the more sure I am of the fact that through customer knowledge salesmen have a golden opportunity to increase their sales figures significantly without any particular expertise in selling, attractive sales personality, or exceptional self-organization.

If all this is true, then why don't salesmen spend more time and effort in gaining more knowledge of their customers and potential customers? The fault, I'm afraid, is largely their managers'. If you find this unpleasant to accept, then please have a look at the forms your salesmen use. Go ahead, look at them right now.

Is there anywhere in that paperwork where a salesman can record any information about his customers apart from such basics as company name, name of contact, date of last visit, and products bought? Where is there a place for him to write in such vital information as his attitude towards our company, which opposition products he buys, his interests and hobbies, or the name of his secretary or assistants? If the forms you provide your salesman with have space for this sort of information, then I congratulate you. If they don't, then don't blame him if he loses sales through lack of customer knowledge.

I usually get two reactions when I talk like this. The first is: why should I spoonfeed my salesmen? If they have any sense at all they will set up their own customer record system, since ordinary file cards will do as well as an official company document. Maybe, but by not having an official company record system, you are virtually telling your men that it isn't important enough for you to bother producing one, so why should they bother to do it? One salesman in a hundred will set up his own system, but he will probably be the crackerjack who doesn't need you anyway.

The other reaction is that while no doubt all that information is valuable, the experienced salesman does not need a special piece of paperwork for it because he carries it in his head; he *knows* all that stuff without having to write it down.

I don't believe it, and neither do you. Take an actual salesman I know who sells coated abrasives. He is a fairly typical industrial salesman. He has 189 customers on whom he calls regularly, 73 of which are resellers and the balance are end-users. He has different calling frequencies for different customers. Some he will not call on more than six times a year, while others must be seen once every week or two. He has a product list of about fifty different abrasives, and some of his customers take as many as thirty of these. He has a different discount structure for different types of customers, and lord help him if he pulls out the wrong price list during a sales call. He has some end-users who use open-coat sanding discs and some who use closed-coat, some who use garnet and some who use emery. This customer has changed over from three-drum sanders to two-drum; that hardware store was given a display rack three months ago and claims it was never delivered; this company is on a cash-with-order basis and if he takes a credit order the credit manager will cry like a baby; the buyer for this concern has been transferred to New Guinea and the new buyer's name is Fotheringham and it is pronounced Futhrim. . . .

And he keeps all that in his *head*?

It is the manager's job to make his salesmen hungry for knowledge, and customer knowledge is a vital part of it. I used to try never to leave a customer of mine without one more piece of information about him that I could put down on my record card, and that is not a bad rule. Even if there were a salesman who could retain all that continuously changing information (if it is not kept up-to-date it is worse than useless), we don't want that information in his head, because what happens when he leaves us? He takes it with him, still in his head. And the new man has to start from scratch.

Every sales team should have engraved in letters of fire in their hearts three principles without which they will never be professionals (I can't afford amateur salesmen and neither can you): know your product, know your enemy, and know your customer.

PLANNING THE SESSIONS

The first question to address in planning the training program is: What are we trying to accomplish? Are these brand new men who need basic overall product training? Are we introducing a new product range to an experienced team? How deeply should we go into the technical side—chemical formulas, pathology, advanced engineering concepts, and so on? If it is refresher training, what are the weaknesses that we need to work on? Get the objectives fixed before you start. All training is expensive, and training without clearly defined objectives is a wretched waste of perfectly good selling time.

With the goals fixed, we now have to decide what form the training will take. The neatest type of training conference is the straight lecture format, with the lecturer reading from his notes, well protected from the group by lecturns and overhead projectors. Neatest, and most dreadfully boring, because this set-up discourages participation and involvement. The trouble is that you are usually stuck with at least *some* lecturing, because it is the quickest way to get a high volume of information across. Even here the good trainer does his utmost to encourage questions and examples from his audience.

Semi-discussion groups, or a panel of trainees talking about certain key points, can be very effective, but these formats assume that the trainees already know the basics. Don't throw a new group into the deep end and expect them to produce a fruitful discussion. It is still necessary for the trainer to lay out the ground rules of the discussion, to keep a relaxed but ever-present hand on the subject matter, and to restart the motor when it stalls. Only in a full-discussion format can he sit back completely out of the picture— and this format can be used only with a mature, experienced, and motivated group.

It is essential to try to measure the success of the training program, both for the benefit of the present group and as a guide for modifying the training for future groups. There is no real substitute for formal tests after the session, and these can be either written or oral. Don't forget that the transmission of product knowledge is actually *teaching,* and you must know how much of the teaching has been absorbed. A good idea is to have two tests, one immediately after the program to judge understanding, and one about three months later to judge long-term retention. There is often a disappointing drop in ratings between the two tests, which bears out the point that training is a never-ending process if your people are to maintain a high level of competence.

WHO SHOULD DO YOUR SALES TRAINING?

So much for teaching, or the acquisition of knowledge. Let us look at training, the acquisition of selling skills. The two have to be well balanced in a salesman, because he must know *what* to say as well as *how* to say it. Here we will deal only with the theoretical, conference room part of sales training. The practical or field training part is so important that it gets a chapter all to itself. The theoretical part concerns what we could call the gentle art of persuasion—the selling process itself. It is not a function of this book to go into the actual syllabus of a sales training course, but there are some points about how to run your sales training that are worth considering before you start spending money on it.

The first question is, do you get an outside whiz-kid in to do it for you, or do you foul it up yourself? There are points for and against both methods. (Aren't there always?) Let us be clear that we are only discussing training in *selling skills*. There is no question about hiring an outside trainer to do your *product* training. This cannot be delegated outside your company. Product training must be done by your own internal people, and it is a sign of weakness if it is done any other way.

In many ways it makes a lot of sense to hire your own full-time sales training man. For one thing, he will then be responsible for both teaching and training, and he can give product knowledge as well as selling skills. Moreover, he can oversee the entire development of each salesman from the time he joins the company, starting with his induction and going right through to advanced training. He can keep close records on each salesman as to the training he has been exposed to and how he has performed in each conference. This in-house man can be very much closer to the real problems of your selling situation. He can go out into the field with the salesmen, getting out to the grass roots, and he can do at least some of the field training itself.

The disadvantages? Really only two. First, the simple one of economics. You need a fairly large sales force to keep a full-time training man fully occupied, and it works out cheaper to pay an outside trainer, even at the outrageous fees which we ask, to come in only when a training course is needed.

The second disadvantage is that training in selling skills is a hell of a lot more subtle and difficult than teaching product knowledge, and if the trainer you hire were really top rate then he wouldn't be working for you, he would be on his own, running training courses two or three days a week and earning a lot more than you could pay him. That sounds brutal, but it isn't meant to be. I, for example, could never do the job that the internal training man does—the painstaking records on each man, the careful follow-up, the constant appraisals—but then, he can't do my job either.

In any case, no good company training manager need be insulted, because in a big enough company he does not actually do very much of the training himself. His job is more the coordinating of the training and development to fit into an overall strategy. He hires people such as me and tells us what he wants, and we jump to his bidding.

Very well, you are going to use an outside agency to do your sales training. Now, whether you pick Michael Beer or whether you decide you need someone better than me, certain points arise:

Beware of the "package deal." This is a course which is made up and offered to all and sundry, no matter what line of selling you are in. The syllabus is rather rigidly structured and does not admit of much change. And because it has to cater to all types of selling situations, it must be done on a rather broad theoretical level. What often happens here is that your salesmen are turned into experts in the theory of salesmanship, and theory never yet got an order signed.

Be wary of any course which relies heavily on films and tapes. This is a similar problem to the one above. The films and tapes were not made for your company, your products, or your problems, and your salesmen, who spend their time trying to sell heavy-duty earthmoving equipment to contractors, may have to sit through a film showing a girl selling a hair dryer to someone's aunt. The proponents of this type of training course will tell you that it doesn't matter, because the basics of selling are the same, whatever you sell. That isn't the point. Certainly the basics are the same, but the basics of the selling process can be given to your men in less than three hours, and anyway, they have heard it all before.

Your salesmen don't want the basics. They want the subtleties of selling *as they apply to their own products,* and they will reject any form of training which does not relate directly to their day-to-day jobs. You have seen this many times. You send them to a lecture, a film, a seminar, and when you ask them what it was like, their reaction invariably is: "It was interesting, but he didn't talk about *my* problems."

Stay away from the "formula" type of training course. There are entire courses comprised solely of acronyms which the salesman has to learn by heart, each letter in the acronym standing for a technique of selling at some stage during the sales talk. He ends up with seven techniques for opening the sale, five for gaining interest, eight for overcoming objections, thirteen for closing the sale, and he is supposed to carry it all around in his head in the form of a formula. From long experience I can assure you that salesmen reject anything in training that looks like a formula, because it simply does not seem to be practical to them. It looks too much like an artificial exercise which has nothing to do with his job in the field. It doesn't matter how good the training is. If the salesman rejects it, then you have wasted your money and, what is much more important, your salesmen's time.

The question of whether to send your men to a commercial sales course or have in-company training is very simply answered. Try by any means you can to run in-company courses. While you can't very well run a proper sales course with two salesmen, as few as five or six can make a good group, big enough for participation and crosspollenation of ideas, and it is vastly better than the best commercial course in the world.

I'm not scorning commercial sales training courses—I run a few every year myself. But when your industrial salesman is sitting in the conference room with a consumer salesman on his left and a fertilizer salesman on his right, he is not going to get any in-depth examination of his particular problems. For example, an industrial man isn't in the least interested in the skills of point of purchase merchandising, but the consumer salesman moves his product mainly by such merchandising techniques and he must spend time on them.

No, if at all possible, in-company training is by far the best. We are talking about in-company *sales* training. For management training it often makes sense to use commercial courses, because generally, with a few exceptions, people problems are people problems, and you will often get very fruitful participation in a group of managers from different companies and industries.

If you do not train your salesmen yourself, do your very best to sit in on the sessions whenever possible, not only to check on how the group is doing but also—and this is a vital point—to show your men that you are not merely paying lip service to their development but are keenly interested in it.

In the final analysis, there is only one criterion of good sales training, and it has nothing to do with the quality of the handout material, the closed-circuit television equipment, the new and dramatic terminology, or the platform personality of the sales trainer. Good training means only one thing and it is this: When you take your hand away from the trainee, when he runs on his own, *is he doing what you trained him to do?*

CONFERENCE ROOM TRAINING TIPS

We end this section with some points on running conference room training sessions, and these apply equally to both teaching product knowledge and training in selling skills:

1. No matter how you run it, your training program is going to cost you far more in time than it is in money: the most expensive part of training is the time lost by having your salesmen off the road. Therefore don't be mean about paying a little more for good meeting facilities. Paying for a good hotel room—rather than crowding into the typists' lunchroom—is money well spent.

2. Start by orienting the group. Get them to introduce themselves and give something of their backgrounds. This will get them used to the idea of talking in the meeting.

3. Explain the objectives of the conference and what you hope to achieve.

4. Explain the form the conference will take, whether it will be run as a lecture, discussion group, panel, role-playing, or some other method.

5. Tell them what you expect from them in the way of feedback and participation. Here you set the tone of the program by showing that each man will have an active part to play. This applies to all but the straight lecture.

6. As soon as possible, find out the level of knowledge, experience, and sophistication of each participant. If you can do this before the meeting so much the better, but it must be done so that you can work at the right level. Too high a level and you will merely bewilder them; too low and you will bore them to tears.

7. The easiest group to handle is the one where the levels of experience are about the same throughout, so try to gather similar levels together at one meeting.

8. Handling the star performer: recognize his worth, defer to his opinion occasionally and indicate that you are "picking his brains." However, never allow him to dominate the meeting and never allow him any special privileges whatever.

9. Handling the lame dog: whatever you do, don't ignore him at question time because this will only reinforce his already low opinion of himself. Ask him questions which will allow him to give an opinion rather than those which admit only of a true/false answer, because here he could make a fool of himself. Get him involved in a discussion where he is on familiar ground. But don't make things too easy for him—he will know what you are doing.

10. People cannot concentrate on a straight lecture for more than twenty minutes at a time. Even your silver-tongued oratory or attractive personality is not proof against mental tuning-out. Break the pace with questions, quizzes, demonstrations—*anything* to stop the boring business of listening to one voice.

A happy thought to take away with you from this section? Here it is: Nobody is ever fully trained. You aren't fully trained, I'm not, and certainly old Chauncey over there isn't. Training is a never-ending process. It *never* stops.

6

The Invigorating Art of Field Training

We are going to have some trouble in this section, partly because I am something of a fanatic about the subject we are about to cover, and partly because so many managers are simply too hide-bound and set in their ways to change. (Not you—those other managers.) Here we examine the art of training the salesman in the field, actually going out with him and making calls, and counseling, demonstrating, and supervising on the job.

There are few things which a manager can do which show such immediate results as field training (if it is properly done), and yet it is a much-neglected management method. Many managers don't do it at all and others do it as little as possible and then in a grudging way.

Why? I wish I had five cents for every time a manager has said to me; "I agree with you one hundred percent about the importance of field training, and I only wish I had the time to do it, but my job keeps me at my desk. Pity." I feel like bursting out at this man, "What is it that you do at your desk that is so damn important that it keeps you out of the field? Please tell me, because it must be very important indeed." Most of the time what he does all day is move papers from his in-tray to his out-tray. Big deal. (I warned you that I was fanatical about this.)

Naturally all managers have administrative responsibilities which prevent their spending very much time away from their desks, but the manager who is directly in charge of a team of salesmen must, *must* arrange his time so that field work forms a significant part of his schedule. If this is impossible, then something is terribly wrong, and it is his responsibility to go to his superiors and have things rearranged to permit him to get the hell away from that desk and out into the field where he can do his men some good.

It would be amusing were it not so tragic how hot and bothered and embarrassed managers become about field training. They say, "I've tried it and it doesn't do any good." One manager even told me pathetically, "I like to go out with my men but they have asked me not to!" What an awful indictment of his management capabilities! Field training is a tremendously useful tool, and merely because we are not skillful at using it is no reason to deny its efficacy. It would be idiotic to claim that there is no virtue in an argon arc welder simply because I can't handle it, but that is what these managers are saying.

Training and supervision in the field is the best way I know to give your salesmen confidence in you as a manager. I have, of course, heard many comments from managers about their salesmen, but some of the comments from salesmen about their managers would split your hangnails right down to your elbow. On the other hand it is heartening to hear a salesman say about his manager, "He isn't just an armchair expert. He comes out with me in rain and shine and *works*. Do you know, he actually got into the window of one of my customers and showed me how to put up a display?" There is nothing I can teach that manager about field training—he's got it.

FIELD TRAINING DON'TS AND DOS

Some points about field training are below, and I see that most of them seem to be "don'ts." Perhaps this is because we do more things wrong than we do right, but anyway:

1. *No more than two people*. It is a sales call you are making, not a deputation. When the customer sees the salesman, his field manager, branch manager, sales director, and some clown from the accounting department marching in in close-order formation, his first reaction is to want to take to the hills. This is a training call and the maximum number is two. (I am not referring to the sort of situation where the top brass is making so-called courtesy calls on customers, where any number can play. This is a *working* call).

2. *It is a normal working day*. Unless the circumstances are really exceptional, nothing should be set up especially for the

manager's benefit. I used to make a practice now and then of telephoning one or another of my salesmen at seven in the morning and saying, "Pick me up in an hour, I'm coming out with you today." There would often be a profound pause on the line and when the answer came it would be: "Uh—*today, Michael*? You know, today isn't really a good day. How does tomorrow grab you?" And that, of course, would make me more determined than ever to make it today, even if it is going to interfere with the mixed doubles he had arranged for this afternoon.

If you ask whether I don't trust my men, the truthful answer is that I don't trust anyone, but that is not the point. It isn't a question of trust. I want to know how he has got his day organized, and this is the only way I can find out. I would not suggest this as a way of life, but it works very well as a change from routine.

3. The call does not belong to you. It is often not an easy thing to accept, but the boss during the sales call is not the manager, it is the salesman. The call belongs to the man who is making it, and if your salesman is the one who is doing the talking, then he is your superior and you are merely taking up space. It must be this way, if only for one reason, namely that the customer will feel that there is something wrong with the call if you give the impression that you are hanging over the salesman's every word and action. Now, doing this is not easy. In most cases the customer knows very well that you are the manager and it can be quite a trick to fade into the background, as it were, but it must be done if you are to give your salesman a fair chance at giving a decent talk.

4. Why are we calling on him? Never allow your salesman to enter the customer's premises without a quick precall analysis. I used to stop my man from getting out of his car and ask, "Just why are we calling on this company?" It sounds like a stupid question, and more than once I have had the answer, "Well, would you believe to try to sell him something?" This is not enough. There has got to be a *reason* for calling, and the reason had better be more to the point than "I always call on him on Thursdays." What did you talk about on the last call here? Did you promise him a brochure which you are now going to deliver? Has he seen a demonstration of the new model FF? Shouldn't he be stocking up for the coming season? Our service people have just been around on a maintenance call: shouldn't we ask him whether he is happy with their work?

There must be a reason for the call, and the time to decide on the reason is *before* we walk in. This allows for proper planning of the talk and prevents the "Hello, Mr. Finkel; I just dropped in to see if you need anything today" approach. Yecch!

5. *Don't grab the club on the downswing.* When your golf swing goes sour on you and you have a lesson with the pro, he will set you up to the ball, get your grip and stance right, and tell you to try a swing. On your backswing he sees that you are still doing something wrong and that the shot you are about to make will be a banana slice. Does he grab the club as you are going into your downswing and make the shot for you? He does not. He lets you make the bad shot and then corrects it afterwards.

You are in a customer's place of business, watching your salesman giving a sales presentation. You see that things are not going very well. Your experience tells you that if the salesman said this or if he did that then the sales talk would have a much better chance of succeeding. Now, what do you do? Do you grab the club on the downswing? Do you brush your man aside and take over the sales talk? If you do, you negate the whole idea of the call. Never forget why you are out with Charlie. You are not there to get orders for him, you are *training* him, and this is a *training* call. Whether or not he gets the order is not so important in itself. What is important is that the call develops him in some way, and a failure can teach him as much as or more than a success. Don't grab the club from him and make the shot yourself; this won't teach him a thing. Let him make the bad shot and show him the right way to do it when the call is over.

Easy to say, hard to do. The temptation is great to take over and get the order. But what have we accomplished? We have gained an order-and lost Charlie a little bit of self-confidence. His reaction will be, "I'm no good. I flounder around and the boss has to wade in and rescue me. It's so easy for him. I will never be as good as that." Great training, that. Another reaction from Charlie, if you persist in taking over the call, will be to lean back every time he gets one small problem in the talk and look at you, and the clear implication will be:

"Okay, you are so damn clever, let's see you handle this one." Again, we gain nothing and lose much.

If all this sounds hard, then let us soften it. Depending on the working relationship you have built up with Charlie, there is surely nothing to stop you, if you see that he has left out an important point in the talk, to put your two cents in as gently as you can: "Excuse me for interrupting, Charlie, but you won't forget to mention the special ads we're placing to promote this product." You then sit back and it is simple for Charlie to go on: "As my boss has just reminded me. . . ." And the damage has been repaired without any blood being shed.

I was covering this point in a seminar of mine and one of the managers was looking very glum about it. I asked him if he disagreed with the point, and he said, "No, Michael, I agree with the principle, but my salesmen sell heavy-duty trucks, and here I am, watching my new salesman talking to a customer whose potential order can be five fifteen-tonners. The talk is going wrong, and he isn't going to get the order. Do I say, 'Well, there goes two months' quota down the drain, but thank goodness, Morris is a bit more developed after today?' " Well, there are exceptions, of course. The point is that Morris as a new salesman should never have been handling an important call such as that. It should not have been a training call at all.

6. *Discuss every call immediately.* As soon as you leave the customer at the end of the call, have a postmortem about it. The postcall analysis is the most important single part of field training, and it should be done right away, before you make the next call. This does not mean a long discussion. It may only amount to: "Good. That was much better, Len. You got your three strongest sales points in and you handled the price resistance very well." This can be done while walking to the next call.

There are times when you will want to go deeper into some aspect of the presentation, and the best place for this is often in the salesman's car. There are three stages to a full postcall analysis:

(a) Ask him how he feels he did. Before you comment on his performance, ask him for his own analysis of his efforts. This is the most painless way to do it, and it builds the habit of self-analysis which is precisely what you want. You will probably find that the salesman is harder on himself than you would be, and this makes the second point easy:

(b) Recognize his strengths. Always try to mention something he is doing well, even if you have to hunt for it. It makes his acceptance of correction much more likely.

(c) Analyze, don't criticize. "Do you think you brought in the aspect of display stands strongly enough? You know, in his business the only way he can move our product is through displays." This is more likely to go down well with the salesman and be incorporated into his next talk than: "You didn't even tell him about the self-sharpening bulldozer blade!" For a new salesman each call can be a traumatic experience, and he doesn't need you to rub his nose in it afterwards.

7. *Be the salesman yourself.* With a brand new, virgin salesman you will of course start by doing the presentation yourself while he watches you with a look of doglike devotion on his face, and only after he has done this for a reasonable length of time will you let him loose on the next unsuspecting customer. However, even when he has found his feet and is making an acceptable presentation, it makes sense to alternate occasionally and be the salesman yourself. This reinforces the point that this is a joint effort.

Opposition to this comes from those managers who say, "But what if I fail in the presentation in front of my own salesman?" Well, now, wouldn't that be a terrible thing? What are we trying to prove—that we are infallible, that we never make a mistake? Certainly we will fail, we will make stupid mistakes. When we leave the customer we do a postcall analysis on ourselves, and we invite the salesman to do the analyzing. He won't think any the less of us. Indeed his reaction is likely to be: "Glory be, my manager is a human being, just like me."

8. *He is worse with an audience.* Realize that he is very conscious of your presence and that you will probably never see your salesman give his best sales talk, simply because you are there. He knows that you know more than he does, that your experience is far greater than his, and that you are listening to every word. Make a discounting in your mind and recognize that tomorrow when he is

on his own he will do better. If he is depressed about his perfor-mance, it is a good thing to remind him of this fact and show him that you are aware of it and that it doesn't bug you, so why should it bug him?

9. *Work a full day.* The exceptions to this are very rare. When you work in the field with your men, work the hours you expect them to work. If you expect them to start at eight and carry on until five, then congratulations—you have just got yourself a nine-hour day. The manager who at three-thirty says, "Well, Bob, I have a lot to do now, so just drop me off at the office and carry on" is not impressing his salesman. Normal reaction from Bob will be: "So the boss if finding it a little too tough to do a full day's calling. Wonder if I can get a couple of frames of snooker in before five o'clock?" There are occasions when you are seeing a few customers with the salesman for a special reason and these calls do not fill your day, but on a training day you stay with him until the bitter end.

10. *Don't neglect the experienced man.* I was once badly shaken when my best salesman said to me, "Hey, am I a typhoid carrier or something? You haven't been into the field with me for nine months!" I looked at him in amazement. "Listen," I said, "the fact that I don't go out with you is a compliment to you. You don't *need* me, and I have three bright young hopefuls on the team who couldn't sell ice on the road to Hades. They do need me, and I am going out with them as much as I can. I fall on my knees in gratitude every morning that I have people like you on the team that I don't have to worry about."

It didn't work. He insisted that I was ignoring him and demanded that I spend an occasional day in the field with him. It took me a while to realize the reason for his attitude: he wanted me to watch him at work and see what a good job he was doing. He wanted, in fact, to be able to do a little mild swaggering in front of me! Well, darn it all, that's not a bad attitude for a salesman to have, and I didn't begrudge the time I spent with him in the field.

Don't neglect your best men. In any case, there is usually some word of advice you can give them, no matter how good they are. If they really are as good as they think they are, then maybe we can learn something from them!

11. Don't let the star do it. On your team you have a star, a natural, a crackerjack salesman, who could make a good living selling canned sand in the middle of the Sahara desert. The temptation is great to send little Steven, your new salesman, out with this man to watch him at work and to learn from him. After all, here is your very best man, and surely it can only be good training for your new men to emulate him.

Don't do it. The star can break the rules, cut the corners, and get away with it. He can do the very things which you have warned Steven not to do, and still make the sale. He doesn't work like us earth people, and putting Steven into his charge could very easily break Steven's spirit. "See how easy it is?" the star asks after coming out of a call where he has sold an automatic milking machine to a wheat farmer (having first persuaded the farmer to plow under his crops and buy cows). "No, I don't!" says Steven in despair.

By all means send your new men out with experienced salesmen. (So long as you realize that you cannot delegate entirely the job of field training. You have to get your own shoes dirty, too.) But pick the salesman carefully. Here is a picture of the man to use, and if you don't have him on your team, then don't use anyone else:

His own sales figures are good. Not necessarily the top producer, he is in the top few.

He works according to the book. He sells in the way your training program recommends.

His paperwork is impeccable.

He is a good team man.

He works a full day.

He doesn't resent being saddled with Steven. If your man doesn't like hangers-on, then for heaven's sake don't give him any, because his attitude will communicate itself to Steven with disastrous results.

In any event, none of this means that you don't have to do the major part of field training yourself. You do.

12. Follow it up. This last point may not apply where you see the salesman every day, but in many cases it is sound practice to follow the training day with a brief note to the salesman. Don't dictate it to your secretary, write it by hand. Thank him for the day, recognize some strengths perhaps, and remind him of any points which came to light during the day. It makes him realize that the day was as important to you as it should have been to him.

FIELD EVALUATION FORM

I want to end this section on field training by giving you something which I created and used when I ran my own group of salesmen. I am not entirely ashamed of it because it seems to work. It may need adaptation to fit your particular selling situation—several of my clients have chopped and changed it to suit themselves—but if you use it, it will make the job of field training a whole lot more productive and meaningful. I call it the "Field Evaluation Form," just to have a name for it, and it is reproduced on page 88. It is used at the end of the day, probably over a beer with the salesman, and it is freely discussed with him. One of its strengths is that it is simple. It takes no more than five minutes to fill in, and ten to discuss with the salesman. It is not a formal appraisal such as we discuss later on in another section. It is not submitted to head office to end up in the saleman's personal file. Nobody ever sees it except the salesman and you. It very effectively shows the salesman exactly how you view his performance during the day, and gives you a basis for discussing how to improve on his weaknesses and build on his strengths.

While the field evaluation is not a formal appraisal, it can be of definite assistance to you when you do your six-monthly appraisal. Instead of having to conjure up opinions from your memory, you have a set of these simple forms in front of you, covering the entire period, and it is easy to see if he has been improving or deteriorating over the period under review. It may sound unlikely, but if these forms are discussed with him in a positive and constructive atmosphere, the salesman actually looks forward to the brief evaluation of the day. Apart from anything else, it seems to give him an insight into what you are trying to do by coming out with him.

If you decide to use it in your own training, by all means change it to suit any special needs of your team, company, or industry, but don't make it any more complicated. Keep it simple and you will probably continue to use it. If you make it a complex document you will probably let it fall into disuse.

FIELD EVALUATION

(For the eyes of the evaluator and salesman only. No copies)

On the 1 to 10 scale, 1 is very poor, 10 is perfect. Less than 4 is well below standard; more than 7 is very good.

Punctuality 10 9 8 7 6 5 4 3 2 1
    Arriving at the meeting place on
    time; reaching appointments on time.

Appearance 10 9 8 7 6 5 4 3 2 1
    Personal, car, samples, literature.

Self-Organization 10 9 8 7 6 5 4 3 2 1
    Properly-planned day.

Economy 10 9 8 7 6 5 4 3 2 1
    No unnecessary mileage, call-backs,
    or expenses.

Product Knowledge 10 9 8 7 6 5 4 3 2 1
Knowledge of Competition 10 9 8 7 6 5 4 3 2 1
Knowledge of Customers 10 9 8 7 6 5 4 3 2 1
Selling Skill 10 9 8 7 6 5 4 3 2 1
    Creating a pleasant opening;
    finding needs; getting sales
    points across; handling resistance;
    getting action.

Paperwork 10 9 8 7 6 5 4 3 2 1
    Keeping customer records up to date;
    filling call reports effectively.

Attitude 10 9 8 7 6 5 4 3 2 1
    Pleasant and positive at all times.

Remarks and Recommendations, Strengths and Weaknesses ————

I am well aware that this section applies mainly to those managers who are directly responsible for a group of working salesmen in the field, and that your job may be several levels above that. In spite of that I urge you to get out from behind that desk as often as you can and go out and get your shoes dirty in the field with salesmen. It can help build the confidence of the sales force in the management team generally and in you in particular, it can give the salesmen's selling effort a new impetus. And if you haven't done it for a long time I promise you that it can be a lot of fun.

7

The Elusive Art of Motivation

Motivation is what it is all about, isn't it? The whole business of managing people is encapsulated in this magic word *motivation*. Millions of words have been spoken and written about it. Scores of theories have been expounded on it. It is the lodestone which all managers seek. It is the most elusive of all the arts of managing people.

Because it is the essence of management, because the man who finally discovers the secret of motivation will gain instant immortality, there has been more nonsense written on this subject than on any other aspect of management, and my first priority in this chapter is an earnest attempt not to add to the pile. If all we manage to do here is clear away some of the rubbish, then at least we are that far ahead.

To give an example of some of the stuff being written on motivation, I read this in a prestigious management journal: "It is not necessary to motivate people. All you have to do is get out of their way so that they can use the tremendous energy and enthusiasm which they bring to their jobs." What is so maddening about reading something like this is that it sounds so good. Damnit, we say, it *must* be true! In fact, it very nearly is true, but the writer (an industrial psychologist) has the truth by the wrong end, as we shall see.

Another theory is the well-known "self-fulfilling prophecy" idea. Here the principle is that whatever you think about your people, you will always be right. If you think that they are lazy, shiftless, and crooked, you will be right because they will conform to your idea of them. If you think that they are industrious, ambitious, and honest, you will also be right because they will strive to live up to your high opinion of them. An interesting theory, and again, so tantalizingly near the truth.

I don't claim to have the secret of motivation. Nobody has it and nobody ever will because motivating people is an art, not a science, and there is no such thing as discovering the secret of an art. Ovid and Beethoven and Chaucer and Leonardo and Wyeth and Donne went a little further than others toward the secret of their callings, but that is all we can say.

Must we discuss whether motivation is an art or a science? Let us dispose of the idea once and for all that it is a science. You will concede that chemistry is a science? Very well. Now, if I put some potassium chlorate and manganese dioxide into a test tube and heat it, I will produce oxygen. I can perform this experiment in London or Paris or Rome or Squaw's Neck, Idaho, and I will always produce oxygen. I state it confidently (I had to look it up), oxygen will always be a product of this experiment. This is because chemistry is a science, and in a science the results of identical actions will always be identical. But let us take a management technique and use it on Ackroyd with excellent results and, confident that we have found the answer, also use it on William.

What will happen? We don't know. We can assume that it will work well because it has worked well in similar circumstances, but we don't *know*. It could blow up in our face, because Ackroyd and William are people, not chemicals, and people are different and react in different ways to identical stimuli.

Art, not science. *Art*.

So what? Why all this fuss over what it is? Art or science, what we are interested in is how to motivate people, not a precise difinition of the word. But it does matter, because when we examine some principles of motivation, as we are about to do, we need to realize that they are not and can never be like the laws of the Medes and the Persians. They are not cast iron rules. Please consider them purely as a basis for further thought, and if they stimulate further thought in your mind, then we shall have accomplished something. In any event, the ideas which follow are mine, and I have been known to be wrong.

Let us then take a few faltering steps along the road to Motivation. Modify them, dispute them, clasp them to your bosom or scrap them altogether.

PEOPLE DON'T MOTIVATE PEOPLE

Whenever I bring out this axiom in a management clinic, I have the feeling that it will be taken as a signal for everyone to stand up and walk out. After all, are we not discussing the motivation of people? If it doesn't exist as a management technique, then what are we doing here? I admit to using the axiom partly for its shock value, but it is strictly true: *People don't motivate people.*

People are not motivated by other people, they are motivated by two concepts only, and they are these: *The wish to gain* good results, *and the wish to avoid* bad results. While these concepts may seem too simple to be accurate, the truth is even more simple than that, because a moment's thought will show that there is only one concept here: *People take action to gain a result.* When someone takes a certain action (and the dictionary definition of motivation is "inducement to take action"), he does so for one reason and one reason only: to gain a desired result or avoid an undesirable one. No one has ever taken any action for any other reason, from Adam eating an apple to man flying to the moon.

To take a few results which motivate people:

Desired results	*Undesired results*
Time saved	Time wasted
Money gained	Money lost
Security	Danger
Prestige	Humiliation
Recognition	Rejection
Leisure	Labor

There can be little doubt that these concepts have motivated people since the beginning of time. *Concepts* motivate people, *results* motivate people—not you or I or any manager on earth.

The results can be divided into "desired" and "undesired" as we have done in the two columns above, but there is another way to divide the same results:

Physical results	Emotional results
Time saved	Peace of mind
Time wasted	Worry
Money gained	Prestige
Money lost	Humiliation
Leisure	Recognition
Labor	Rejection

Here we have ignored the wanted or unwanted aspects of the results and have split them into physical, tangible results and emotional, intangible results. Again, they are motivating forces.

Where are we after all this? We are here: You cannot force a man to be successful. It is his own desire to be successful, to gain the result he wants, which makes him take the actions to ensure that success.

Sit back now and think of one of your salesmen, preferably an average or even mediocre performer. Can you force him to be a success at the job? You can force him to carry out your instructions, simply by holding over his head the threat of dismissal. You can make him call on the required number of customers, make him go through a prepared sales sequence, make him produce regular call reports. Will this make him successful? No, of course it won't. You have not motivated him, you have merely forced him to go through the motions.

Now, if we accept that we don't motivate our people, what on earth can we do as managers? *We can show the results of taking actions*. And we can do this so logically, convincingly, and persuasively that he says to himself, "My God, the boss is right! If I do what he suggests I will gain the very results I want, I will be able to do what I have always yearned to do!" And he grabs the ball and runs with it.

Certainly, he would not have taken the action unless we had spoken, but the motivation came not from our talk but from his desire for the result. Had he not had that desire, we could talk until birds began nesting in our hair without achieving a single thing. He has to have the spark—we cannot create it. If he does have the spark, then we can blow on it and produce the bright clear fire of motivation, but the spark must be there first. All we can do is point out the result of taking the action. If that result is not attractive to him, if it does not fan the spark into a small flame, then not the silver tongue of Demosthenes will change him by one iota.

May I give you a simple example of this from my own household? I love my two daughters dearly. They are intelligent, decorative, and a credit to their mother and to the cosmetic industry. I get on very well with them, but I cannot pretend that they are much use around the house, since they have a psychological block about picking up anything they have dropped, switching off anything they have switched on, or closing anything they have opened. Delightful girls in many ways, but considered purely as useful beings, they leave something to be desired. A bone of contention has always been the state of their bathroom. They emerge from the bathroom, resembling the front cover of a beauty magazine, but the bathroom itself looks very much like a scene from a big-budget disaster movie.

Suppose I wish to motivate them to pick up their towels and generally clean up a little. There are various ways I can go about this:

"Clean up your bathroom, and I'll raise your allowance." (No result, either because they have enough money for their present needs or because the idea of doing something for financial reward has not yet occurred to them as a way of life.)

"Clean up your bathroom. It looks like a pigsty." (Its *our* bathroom and, anyway, what has Daddy got against pigs? They're nice animals.)

"Clean up your bathroom or I'll clobber you!" (Since we have never operated on the clobbering principle the reaction would be: Daddy is being funny again.)

"Clean up your bathroom. If you don't, Mummy will have to do it, and she has had a tough enough day already." (The bathroom is immediately cleaned up.)

And I might feel that I had done an effective job of motivating them. Did I really? No. They were motivated by the wish to avoid an unwanted result—in this case, the extra work which their mother would have to do. All I did was to point out the result of taking action. Now, if they had had no affection and regard for their mother, my message would have fallen on deaf ears, so in fact it was this affection which motivated them.

Only for the sake of convenience do we talk about motivating people. I shall be doing it in this chapter, but it is the very cornerstone of good management to recognize that people don't motivate people, they merely point out the result of taking action, and if the result is desired enough then the action will be taken. When we say about a man, "I simply can't motivate him, no matter what I say or do," we are saying that we have failed to find the spark in him to blow on.

EVERYBODY WORKS HARD AT SOMETHING

The Spanish have a saying: *Todo hombre tien algún aspecto de honor* (each man has some sort of honor). Even the biggest blackguard in the world has something he holds sacred. Right, and even the most idle wastrel in the world is prepared to work hard at *something*. That salesman of yours who stares out of the window at sales meetings, who attends the matinees three days a week, and who spends valuable selling time drinking coffee with the boys—he is actually capable of hard, sustained effort. The trouble is merely that you are not getting any of that effort, but he can produce it for *something*. Follow him home and you may find to your amazement that he works very hard indeed as unpaid secretary of the local child welfare organization; that he is working his fingers down to nubs helping a friend to build a boat; that he spends his weekends up to his hips in compost, covered in flies and sweat. He is capable of effort, and getting him to give some of that effort to the job we are paying him to do is known as motivation.

Here is an example which I love to tell because for once I did something dramatically right. I had a salesman whose product was office machines. He was not very good, not very bad, just very medium. He had ability but not very much motivation, and I had tried to find his spark with only limited success.

One day he started talking about his daughter who was, according to him, a future Margot Fonteyn. Ballet was her whole life and her teachers were enthusiastic about her potential. She desperately wanted to go overseas to London to further her studies. He said gloomily, "Of course, that's a dream. No way can I afford to send her." I said, "Of course, you can send her." He shook his head. I said, "I'm telling you, Chris, you can send her!"

He looked at me as though I had said he could melt the polar icecaps. I got on the phone and found out the price of the cheapest fare to England on a go now, pay later basis; I learned from Chris that there were friends she could stay with over there; I phoned my wife for an estimate of what the fees for the ballet school would be (she knows useless things like that); Chris and I figured out what she would need as a monthly allowance; I wrote it all down and showed it to him.

He looked surprised. "Less than I thought," he said. "Still too much for me, though." I said, "Based on your present commission scale, how many more machines would you have to sell each month to reach that figure?" It was as though a light had gone on inside him. "Three," he said. "Only three!" He nearly knocked my desk over getting up from his chair. "I gotta get home. I gotta get home!"

Believe me, that's *motivation.*

IDENTIFYING MOTIVATIONAL CAPACITIES

Here are two salesmen, call them citizen A and citizen B. Citizen A has a comparatively small capacity for motivation. His needs are few, his desires are largely being satisfied. Citizen B has a much larger capacity for motivation. There is something big he wants but doesn't have—indeed, now that he thinks about it, he wants nearly everything—and he can be motivated to work like the dickens to get those things. Considering this we would be inclined to say that citizen A is probably loafing on the job while citizen B is doing a relatively good job of work.

Not necessarily. Each one's *actual* motivation, as opposed to their potential motivation, may tell quite a different story. While citizen A's "motivation tank" may be full almost to capacity, citizen B's may be almost empty. Therefore it is likely that citizen A is doing an acceptable job, working to full capacity, and citizen B is the one who is spinning his wheels. Since their capacities for motivation are very different, you would handle these two citizens in very different ways.

Citizen A   Citizen B

Take citizen A first. This man has always interested me. You recognize him, don't you? You undoubtedly have a citizen A in your team. He has a limited capacity for motivation, but he is operating at about the full level of that capacity. He will never rise very high in your company because he will never get much more motivated than he is now. He is the hewer of wood and the drawer of water—and you need him.

Every organization on earth has its citizen A's, and they are vital to the running of the business. They are the middle-aged salesmen, the reliable senior clerk, the steady technician. Handling him is not an overly complex affair. You will recognize good performance, give him his salary increases as they are justified, make sure that his working conditions are as good as possible, and simply let him get on with the job. He is doing an acceptable level of work for an interesting reason. His work means really only one thing to him and that is the piece of long green paper which he gets every month *and which allows him to do those things which are far more important than his job.* His job does not mean anything significant in his life except as a means to an end, and he sees it only as a way to have that vine-covered cottage, to belong to the swim club, to enjoy those fishing trips with the boys.

Could he ever become a citizen B? Yes, but it would mean a complete change in his attitude, and don't think that his manager is likely to accomplish this. His own circumstances would have to change, and this would have to come from within him. It is possible that I managed to change the ballet dancer's father from a citizen A to something approaching a citizen B, but that was unusual and I didn't do it myself; it was his own desire that did it. All I did was fan the flames.

If it sounds as though I am sneering at the citizen A's of this world, I'm not. In an odd way I am one myself. I have little personal ambition to make a name for myself in the corporate business world, which is why I pulled out of the mainstream of line management and found a job on the sidelines. I am capable of working very hard indeed, but this is only so that I can, as it were, buy the leisure to watch a few sunsets, enjoy my daughters growing up, play mediocre golf, and toast with good friends the wide-screen tragicomedy of life.

But what of citizen B? Handling him is a very different matter, and it is vitally important, because while you need citizen A to hew the wood and draw the water, it is citizen B who is going to make you rich and famous as a sales manager. If your own citizen B's are already motivated up to their capacities, then fall on your knees in thanks and ensure by every means you can that they are kept happy in their jobs.

On the other hand, a citizen B who has a large capacity but whose present level of motivation is low is the real test of your management abilities. This man is the reason you are in your present job. It's true. Your company put you where you are so that you could identify this man and fill that motivational reservoir to its capacity.

First, how do we identify him? How do we distinguish between him and a citizen A? There is no easy way, and, to be honest, sometimes we don't ever succeed in identifying him. Instead we fail with him, and he leaves the company and perhaps finds a better manager elsewhere. The only way to identify him is to talk to him, counsel and appraise him, try to get inside him and find out what makes him tick.

Easier said than done. You do not have a psychoanalyst's couch in your office and, besides, you do not have the expertise or the time to go into depth analysis of your man. Still, it is astonishing how much comes out in simply talking. My most fruitful chat sessions with salesmen have been in their cars, going with them from call to call. Away from the official atmosphere of the office, on a man-to-man basis, your man will often open his heart to you and show you what he is, what he wants from life, what his motivational potential could be. Whether you can do this sort of thing depends on your working relationship with your men. Many managers simply never have the knack for it, and they lose the opportunity of getting inside their men and creating the climate in which self-motivation can take place.

THREE ESSENTIALS FOR A MOTIVATED STAFF

We have already made the point that people differ. Now we must recognize that in some fundamental ways they are the same. All people need certain things from their work, and the following three points try to show this, each one illustrated by an example.

In a large company which made and sold office furniture, the top management group met each month to examine sales figures, stock held, back orders, and so on. These data came from the branches and were collated by a woman clerk who held a key position in the firm. She enjoyed the work although the job of getting all the information together was complex and time consuming. She knew that without her there would be no management meeting because there would be no figures to examine.

Then the company began using the services of a computer bureau which produced all the required information with the split-second speed and insolent accuracy of all computers. By the horrible sort of breakdown in communication which occasionally happens even in the best of companies, nobody told the clerk that her figures were no longer needed, that what had taken her over a week to do was now being done by a few silicon chips in about forty-five seconds. She actually went on doing the job for three months before she learned the truth. Her reaction was immediate and violent: she resigned on the spot and within a week had had a nervous breakdown. The point?

> *People need to feel that their work is useful. To destroy motivation, show a man that his work contributes nothing.*

This is an age of industrial strikes. In almost all cases the strikers walk out for more money, and because we have allowed things to get to the stage where a shop steward with a hangover can single-handedly bring a huge organization to a halt, the money is usually forthcoming, and the workers go back to their lathes and drill presses.

Are they any happier? No, they are not—because the money was in most cases not the real reason for the strike. The real reason is that when a man spends his entire lifetime drilling the same three holes in the same chassis member of the same goddamned washing machine, he eventually realizes that nobody notices, nobody cares; that if he fell over dead they would prize the drill out of his senseless fingers and give it to somebody else—and noboby would give a damn.

The strike is not for more money, better retirement benefits, or a longer coffee break. It is a despairing scream from this man and ten thousand others: "Recognize me! I am an important human being, but while I am working you don't even know that I exist—now see what happens when I stop!" The point?

> *People need recognition of their worth, and their continued worth to the company depends largely on that recognition.*

For an example of the third point come, with me on a trip away from my home base. I had checked into my hotel and had wandered into the bar for a drink before dinner. I began a casual conversation with the man next to me who turned out to be a salesman. He mentioned the name of his company and I was immediately interested because I had recently met the sales director of that company, and he had impressed me as being a man of iron, a strict disciplinarian with little sense of humor, and generally a tough potato. I said to my drinking partner, "Isn't your boss Mr. Whosis?" He nodded. "What's he like to work for?" I asked, quite unforgivably, but anyone engaged in basic research must wear a hard outer shell.

He told me what his boss was like. He showed a fine feeling for words as he traced his ancestry back to the serpent in the Garden of Eden through Ivan the Terrible, Attila the Hun, and Abdul the Damned. He went back over his past sins, and forward to his certain destination after death. When he finally ran down I said, "You know, you interest me. I have been talking to you for a while and you come over very well. You could obviously get a job anywhere.

Why do you continue to work for a man who has all the, uh, deficiencies you describe?" He said nothing for a while and I became concerned that I had been too intrusive, but he was merely trying to put his thoughts into words.

"I'll tell you," he said. "It's true that he's unreasonable, he expects too much, he blows up at the slightest thing, and when he leans on you, you know you've been leaned on. But I always know where I stand with that man. And he knows exactly where he's going."

This was the reason he gave for continuing to work for a tough guy: I always know where I stand with him, and he knows where he is going. The point?

People need motivated and consistent leadership, and they will forgive a man almost anything if he provides it.

You cannot expect a motivated team if you yourself are not highly motivated, and motivation is a very difficult thing to fake; your men will see through you every time. On the other hand, history is filled with examples of men who by their own high motivation have imbued their people with the same spirit. While your job as manager of a group of salesmen selling rust-proofing compounds may not be as glamorous as Scott in the Antarctic or stout Cortez upon a peak in Darien, the principle is the same.

LIGHTING YOUR SALESMAN'S FIRE

Earlier in this chapter I said that it is a cornerstone of good management to realize that people don't motivate other people. Rather, all we can do is point out the results of taking action and if the results are desirable enough (or bad enough), if you strike the right spark, action will be taken.

If motivation is "inducement to take action," then you have to decide what action you wish your salesman to take—and what the desirable results will be—before you go about inducing it. Generally, of course, you want your man to carry out his duties as outlined in his job description. Specifically, you may want him to organize his working day better, to pay more attention to costs, to gain a better knowledge of his customers, to concentrate on a slow-moving line, or to produce better paperwork—it depends on the exigencies of the moment or on long-term objectives for the future.

Forcing him to do these things merely makes him go through the motions, doing the absolute minimum to keep you off his back. This is not inducement to action and it is therefore not motivation. *Convincing* him to do these rather everyday things (let's face it, they come with his job)—well, you'll just have to use those finely honed sales skills that got you where you are today. Convincing him to do those things comes with *your* job.

Okay, so he's doing his job well enough, but how do you keep his enthusiasm up, how do you inspire him to perform with that extra something that we would call true motivation? Here are random examples of some tricky motivational situations that almost inevitably occur among a sales team. These situations will truly test your talent for inducing action. They are also examples of situations where *selling* him on the idea instead of *telling* him to do it will prove the more effective way.

Your salesman may have lost faith in himself. Everyone has ups and downs, and because of the peculiarities of the job of selling this happens more often and more intensely to salesmen than to others. You may have to show him that he is just as good as he was in his recent "up" time, that the law of averages will work for him if only he will keep the quality of his effort at a high level.

If his attitude is hindering his progress, it may be necessary to point this out without mincing your words. Many people are more influenced by the wish to avoid unwanted results than by the wish to gain wanted results, and sometimes the motivation is best engendered by pointing out the unwanted consequences which could occur, using very firm language indeed.

One of the most effective ways to point out the results of taking action is to take the action yourself, to demonstrate. This is motivation by example, and it is used by the best leaders of men. You wish him to do something in his daily job better than or differently from the way he is doing it now? Go out into the field with him and demonstrate that it can be done. This is practical motivation at its best.

Many men respond well to challenge. Show me what others in my position and with my problems have done, and it will spur me to emulate or better their efforts.

A subtle and difficult type of motivational skill is needed when the salesman gets the feeling that he is in a dead-end job with nothing to look forward to over the years but more of the same dreary round of calling on the same dreary customers. This happens to most salesmen at one time or another. It is a legacy from the time when a man became a salesman because he was too stupid to be a doctor or a lawyer, and the built-in feeling of inferiority is still there in some of us salesmen.

The salesman who is suffering from this disease may have the ability to grow, in which case your motivating influence could take the form of educating him into realizing that his future with you is bright but that patience is needed. He will not be satisfied with empty promises, though, and in any case promises are dangerous. You will have to spell it out for him in concrete but realistic terms.

But what if he lacks the ability to grow further, if you do not see him as promotoble material? It takes a good deal of moral courage to tell a man that while he is a valued member of the team, and that continued good work on his part will ensure that he will always earn a comfortable living, you believe that he has got as far as he is going. This honest and straight talking may reinforce his own low opinion of himself, and if clumsily done it may have a negative effect. On the other hand, often when the truth is pointed out in this way he accepts it and becomes a worthwhile citizen A. He stops striving for something out of his reach and plugs away contentedly at the job he knows he can do adequately. He limits his personal horizons.

It may be remarked that inducing a man to restrict his reach is hardly motivation. I think it is. You are fitting him into the slot which suits him and making him a happy and productive person at the level at which he operates best. And if that isn't motivating, then what is?

A SUMMARY

That's about it on motivation. Perhaps all we have done here is clear away some of the gobbledygook that is so freely thrown around on the subject, but even so we are that much ahead. It is worthwhile summarizing briefly:

1. *We don't motivate people.* People are motivated by the wish to satisfy basic inner needs. If you can't find these needs, then you will

never motivate them, and you have the wrong people. The solution is to gather around you people who have needs which you can find and awaken to life.

2. *Everybody works hard at something.* Again, finding what is important to a man is the only sure way to get him to motivate himself. If his whole life is his daughter's interest in ballet, then quit trying to get him to sell office machines, and talk about his daughter. Make him *see* her taking the lead at the Royal Command Performance and the Queen coming backstage. You think that's corny? So do I. But Chris doesn't.

3. *Motivation differs in different people.* Recognize the citizen A's on your team and don't bust yourself trying to motivate them to citizen B's. Find the citizen B and motivate the hell out of him.

4. *People need to feel that their work contributes.* We go deeper into this when we discuss human relations, but for now, if you do everything you can to show each man how his work fits into the big picture, you will go a long way to creating a motivating climate.

5. *Recognize personal worth.* This is tied to the previous point, but it goes further. Realize that every one of us is silently screaming at the world, "Look at me! I am an important person!"

6. *People need consistent and motivated leadership.* If you are motivated yourself (truly motivated, not merely kidding yourself), then much of what we have been discussing here will come easily to you. If you are not motivated in your present job then you are in the wrong job, so find another line of work.

Go even part of the way along the road we have been exploring in this chapter and you will be building a truly motivated team. *Then* all you will need to do, as the industrial psychologist said in the beginning of this chapter, is get out of their way and let them use the tremendous energy and enthusiasm which they will bring to their jobs.

8

The Crucial Art of Communicating

I suppose that if we were to pick one talent common to all the famous figures of history from Aristotle to Churchill it would be their ability to communicate. Think of anyone you like—Henry V, Joan of Arc, Lenin, Billy Graham. The one shining gift they all had was the ability to set the hearts of men on fire. The entire story of mankind is highlighted by people who through the use of words— exactly the same words which we use every day—changed the minds and attitudes of their listeners, changed defeats into victories, changed the lives of millions.

All right, so you don't want to win the battle of Agincourt, liberate France, head a revolution, or save souls. But you do want to manage people, and if you were a better communicator you would be a better manager. The point is that communicating does not only mean *explaining*. Communicating means *persuading, changing concepts,* and much of management hinges precisely on those skills.

Managing people means influencing them, affecting their thoughts and actions in some way. Now, there are only three ways that we can influence people: how we look, what we do, and what we say.

You can't do very much about how you look and, anyway, this is the least effective way of influencing people. What you do is obviously important—and the rest of this book is concerned with that.

This chapter is concerned with what we say. It is only one chapter because this is all I know about communication, but I suggest that you read it several times. It will repay the effort many times over. If it helps to make you a better communicator then you are ahead of the game, because most people are such terrible communicators that you will be in an elite minority.

Permit me to read your mind at this very moment. Right now, you are saying to yourself, "Well, actually, thank heaven, communication is one thing I don't have very much trouble with. I express myself pretty well, come to think of it. This section is for the bad communicators. I guess I'll just skip it and go on to something I do need help on." If you are a normal sort of person, then that is probably close to what is going on in your mind. Well, isn't it? That would be a normal reaction, and it is the most dangerous mistake we make about communication. The biggest problem with us communicators is that we think, "I am good at *communicating*. You are bad at *understanding*."

ADMIT YOU'RE NOT THAT GREAT AT IT

There is the story of the man who taught himself German using language tapes and then decided to take a holiday in Germany. On his return his friends asked if he had had any difficulty with his German. "Not at all!" he said. "No difficulty whatever! Mind you, those Germans—*they* had some difficulty with it."

All of us believe that we communicate well enough and the trouble is with those other people who don't understand, won't listen, or are too stupid. That is the problem, friend, and until you take a deep breath and admit that you are not a good communicator, you don't stand much chance of ever becoming one. Go on, take the divine leap right now and say to yourself, "I am a poor communicator." Once you have done that you are at least on the road toward becoming a better one.

Need an example of how easy it is to communicate poorly? I was on an aircraft recently and accepted the dinner tray handed to me by the stewardess. Lord knows what process airlines use to turn perfectly good food into the dreadful stuff they offer you, but I happened to be hungry enough to face it. When I had eaten all I could handle, the stewardess came down the aisle, carefully balancing an unstable load of empty trays, and reached to take mine. I hesitated to give it to her and even asked, "Can you manage another tray?" She looked at me a little sideways and said, "Sure!" Well, she disappeared down the aisle and blow me down if she didn't come back in three minutes with a fresh tray of food!

Now, this example was no big deal, and the only bad result was that I had to choke down another dinner because I lacked the moral courage to tell the stewardess that she had misunderstood me. But when we think about it, our lives are full of little failures in communication such as this, and if we can't communicate in the trivial situations, then how are we going to do in the important ones?

> *Where there is willing cooperation, where the listener wants to understand and where he does not understand, then there is only one dunce in that twosome and it is the communicator, not the listener.*

I have a fine example of the above point. When creating a sales training clinic for a new client, one question I ask the sales manager is, "What is the biggest single problem your salesmen face in the field?" I asked this question of the sales director of a company which sells bituminous compounds for roadbuilding and his answer came back promptly. "It's the darned distributors," he said. "If we could get the distributors working effectively we wouldn't have half the troubles we have."

I knew what he meant, of course. When you sell your products through distributors or wholesalers who handle many lines in addition to yours, much of the fine edge of your selling effort can be lost. "I see your problem," I said. "How would it be if we got the distributors to sit in on the seminars? It sounds as though they could use some sales training."

He looked at me as though I had sprouted another nose. He said, "Mr. Beer, what the *hell* are you talking about?" He fished in his desk and threw me a photograph of one of those huge machines which waddle down the road spewing bitumin from a hundred nozzles at the rear. "That is a distributor. Just how do you propose to get it into a conference room and train it?"

Well, we straightened out the misunderstanding, but he was

probably left with the impression that I was pretty unknowledge-able. Maybe I am, but you couldn't prove it by that episode. The only unperceptive person in that interchange was the sales director. Used in that context, the word *distributor* was a technical term perculiar to his specific industry, and he should have realized that using it without explanation to a layman was very poor communication.

Tired of examples? Well, here's another. But this time it's of *good* communicating. My barber has two razors on his shelf, one with a white handle and one with a black, which he uses to get rid of the odd bits of fluff at the back of my neck. I had noticed that the black-handled razor always seemed to be really sharp whereas the white one always left me with an irritating razor burn. One day as he was reaching for a razor I said, "Carlo, you know why I always come to you? Your razors are the sharpest in town." He grinned with pleasure and said, "You bet!"—and reached for the black razor. Not only do I always get the black razor now, but Carlo shaves my neck as though he was taking the fuzz off a peach. When he is through, he says, "Razor sharp enough?"

Now that is *communication!* Without complaining about the blunt razor, without telling him to use only the sharp one, I got him to give me the best neck shave in town. And he does it with pride and pleasure, because he *wants* to do it. That is one fundamental of effective communication, namely that people do what you want them to do because they also want to do it.

So, if communication is so vital to management, then it is necessary that we become expert in the art. How expert you can be depends on your personality. You have basic characteristics which will help you to communicate well, such as a feeling for words, an attractive presence, an "honest" face (don't knock it, it helps). You may have some defects which will hinder your way to good communication, such as a difficulty in translating ideas into words, a nervous manner, a mumbly way of talking, or halitosis. In spite of these, you can be a better communicator, and this skill can help you every day, all through your life, in small ways as well as big ones. It will help you in the business of managing a sales team and in situations far removed from that.

Okay, let's turn you into as good a communicator as you can possibly be. Practice what follows, become skillful at it, and people will listen, applaud, agree, and obey.

EXAMINE YOUR PREJUDICES

You don't like me, my clothes, my accent, the color of my skin, my manner? If your prejudices unduly influence your reactions to me, then the moment you try to communicate with me I will sense your ill feeling. Personal dislike is very difficult to disguise. Your antipathy will come through in the way you talk, in the way you shake my hand, in the way you use your eyes.

Antipathy breeds antipathy. My reaction will be, "Who does he think he is? He's no first prize himself!" When I feel that you don't like me, I immediately find things about you to dislike, and I have no trouble finding those things. What happens then is that we both begin to build walls between us, and communication will be extremely difficult, if not downright impossible.

Now I am not saying that you should get rid of your prejudices. If you have an unreasoning dislike of Irishmen, red hair, left-handed people, or suede shoes you will continue to feel this way no matter what anyone says. Our prejudices are very precious to us, and we relinquish them reluctantly if at all. But we do need to recognize that the dislike we feel is irrational. We need to acknowledge that we don't have to like someone but we have to communicate with him, and we must handle the situation, if not with amity, then at least with diplomacy.

I was present at a sales interview between a pharmaceutical salesman and a physician. The salesman was, if you are on his side, with it and switched on in his dress and manner. If you are against him, then his hair was longer than Rapunzel's and his clothes looked like test night in a Chinese firework factory. The physician, on the other hand, was austere and ascetic in appearance and manner.

The interview was not going well. The salesman was describing a new way of sterilizing the operating area in abdominal surgery, and the doctor was obviously so put off by personal factors that he was not paying attention to the technical details of the talk. At length the salesman stopped in mid-sentence and said, "Doctor, I can see that you don't like me. I'm sorry about that, because I respect you and admire what I have heard about your work. It would be a pity if your feelings towards me prevented you from learning about this new technique, because I know that it will be of real help to you."

The doctor looked at the salesman very hard for a moment and then said, "Very well. Go on." From then on he listened and the interview went much better. As we were leaving he cleared his throat and said, "I don't dislike you, my boy," and he damn nearly smiled!

What the physician did not realize was that the salesman was as prejudiced as he was. When we were safely out of the office the salesman grinned and said, "What a stuffed shirt he is!" But he had suppressed his prejudices in order to communicate.

You don't like me? I'm sorry about that. But recognize the problem and be prepared to temporarily suppress your prejudices. Never mind liking me, *communicate* with me!

CLARIFY THE ISSUES

Think it through first. An elementary point, not even worth listing? Maybe, but many failures in communication stem from a failure to ask ourselves, "Exactly what is the problem, idea, information, or instruction that I wish to get across?" Instead of backing away and taking a little time to think through what we are trying to achieve, we jump on our horse and charge—and fail.

You are a member of the financial division of your company. Oh, come on, be honest—you are an accounting clerk. Humbert at the next desk has got into the habit of holding on to certain returns until he has a nice big pile before he processes them. The trouble is that this holds up your work and you often have to work overtime when Humbert finally hands them over to you. You take this as long as you can, and when the tide of resentment finally rises too high you burst into your boss's office. "Humbert is bugging me," you say. "He has no consideration for other people. Because it suits him I have to work overtime. You should do something about him!"

Well, that is a great piece of communication. Not only does your boss not have the faintest idea what you are talking about, but he has also added up in his computerlike mind several interesting facts about you: (1) you can't get on with the rest of the team; (2) you resent a bit of overtime, (3) you're a clock-watcher; (4) you are a whiner who can't sort out his own personal problems.

Great communication, hey? And so unnecessary if only you had cleared it in your own mind first, had asked yourself exactly what it was you wanted to achieve. Then, it might have come out something like this:

"We have a small problem which is holding up the month-end returns. I am getting them from Humbert in big batches and this makes it difficult to get them through to you in time. I know that Humbert is busy, but do you think that he could process them as he gets them and pass them to me immediately? This would speed it up all along the line."

That's communication. The problem is clearly defined, a solution is suggested, and no personality hassles are dragged in. Think about this for a moment. Isn't it true that when you have failed to communicate it has often been because, without clarifying the issues first, you have attacked the *person* rather than the *problem*?

DRAW A PICTURE

If you can draw a picture, then half your communication problems will disappear. Well, maybe a third. People think in pictures, not in words. It doesn't matter how intelligent or sophisticated the listener is, he still thinks in pictures. I'll prove this to you, since you probably don't think that great minds such as Einstein or Edison or Copernicus thought in pictures. You are fairly intelligent? Good. Then read this:

Eiffel Tower   Pineapple   Giraffe   Epistaxis

You have a picture of each of these in your mind, don't you? You can *see* the fretwork silhouette of the Eiffel Tower, the spiky top of the pineapple, the awkward grace of the giraffe, the—ah, well, unless you have had medical training you probably have no *pictures* of epistaxis. There is nothing to think about when you see the word;

it throws nothing on your mental TV screen; you can't picture it. Do you believe now that we all think in pictures? (It's a nosebleed, you dim-wit.)

So if we think in pictures, then the most immediately dramatic and effective way to communicate is in pictures. But I don't mean pictures of trees and clouds and flowers; I mean charts, diagrams, graphs. You can't always communicate with a pencil and paper, but when you can (and that's oftener than you think) you have little difficulty in making yourself understood.

When multigrade motor oil first came on the market I explained how it worked to a group of salesmen. Their only question when I had finished explaining the technical points was, "How much is it going to cost?" I went into the field with one of the salesmen soon after this and all my teeth turned black when I heard him say to a customer, "This new multigrade oil is the greatest! When you put it into your cold engine it's thin, just like water, and when the engine heats up the oil gets thicker and thicker!"

Michael Beer, the great communicator. I called another sales meeting and announced that I was going to explain multigrade oil to them. "You told us about that last week," I was reminded. "Well, I'm going to tell you again this week," I snarled. I drew two lines on the blackboard, then I put another line across the graph:

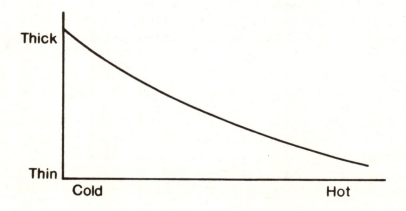

I said, "See? That's ordinary motor oil. When it's cold, it's thick; when it's hot, it's thin." "Sure," the group said. "We know that." "Do you also know this?" I asked, and drew another line:

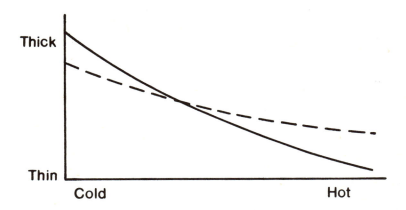

"That is multigrade oil. When it's cold, it's not so thick as ordinary oil, and when it's hot, it's not so thin." "Now why didn't you tell us that last week?" "I'm sorry," I said. "I thought I had, but I was wrong."

Four lines on a blackboard communicated something which a lot of words failed to do. This is why some highly technical people can communicate so well. You know the engineer who reaches for a pencil and paper when you ask him how to get to the post office? He is probably a good communicator because he is used to translating ideas into pictures.

Draw a picture. You will be amazed at how many thoughts can be put on paper in this way. Try explaining to your wife how much of the monthly budget goes on food, how much on light, insurance and clothes, and she will probably fall asleep halfway through your speech. Show her the ratios of one expense to the other by using a pie chart and it all suddenly falls into place. A pie chart? Hell, everybody knows what a pie chart is! It's a round thing with lines which. . . .

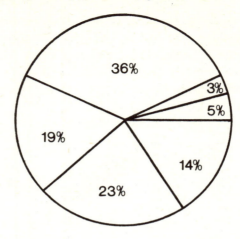

Okay, now we *all* know what a pie chart is.

SPEAK THE LISTENER'S LANGUAGE

If you can successfully speak your listener's language then the other half of the problem of gaining understanding will disappear. By speaking the listener's language I don't mean talking Italian if his name is Guiseppe or Swahili if his name is M'wangi. I mean using terms, expressions, and analogies which he will readily understand because they are part of his daily experience, because they are ones he uses himself.

If there is one cause of poor communication more important than any other, then this is it. We fail to realize that words mean different things to different people, that an expression which you have used automatically all your life is either completely meaningless to me or else means something entirely different to me.

The words we choose can have serious consequences. They can have hidden meanings; they can be "loaded" to sound friendly or hostile. Take the word *guerrilla*, for instance, which is Spanish for "little war." It refers to a person who fights in irregular skirmishes outside the conventions of normal warfare. The word is neutral in itself; it has no connotation either for good or for bad (at least to me it doesn't), and as a description of the members of, say, the Palestine Liberation Organization it will do very well, *if* you have no special feelings about that organization.

But what if you are an Arab? You might want to express your admiration for the activities of the PLO. "Guerrilla" by itself won't do this, so you might call them "freedom fighters." If you are an Israeli, then the word "guerrilla" would also not express your feelings towards these people, and you would most likely change it to "terrorist."

Three terms, all describing the same activity: one neutral, one friendly, one hostile. Where does it lead us? Well, to take a rather extreme example, you would be a brave man to make a speech in Tel Aviv about the Middle East problem and refer to the PLO as freedom fighters. Even "guerrilla" would not make you many Israeli friends.

Incidentally, if that example sounds unrealistic, a prominent member of the British Government some years ago distinguished himself by appealing to the Arabs and Jews to try to settle their differences in "a spirit of *Christian* charity." Incredible, yes, but that is what happens when we don't speak the listener's language, when we look at things from our point of view only, when we use words which are friendly, neutral, or familiar to us instead of to those we wish to persuade or influence.

Selecting words properly is not easy. We are so used to the way we use words that it is difficult to remember that words can be dangerous weapons, that they must be carefully handled. Constant vigilance is required to avoid antagonizing people. When I was first promoted from the sales force, my job was assistant sales manager. I was directly in charge of a group of salesmen, responsible for overseeing their territory coverage, their sales figures, setting quotas, and so forth. In fact, I was to all intents and purposes the sales manager. Yet this company in its wisdom had decided that my official title should be "sales assistant."

Imagine it. Here I was proud of being selected for promotion, determined to do the very best job I could, and I was landed—branded—with a title which sounded as though I sold soap and shoe polish from behind a shop counter! I did not stay in the company long and indeed my main reason for leaving was the feeling that if all they thought of the level of my job was to label it "sales assistant," then the hell with them.

Does this sort of thing seem trivial to you? It isn't. That title was hostile and denigrating, although I am sure that it was not meant to be, and it caused unnecessary resentment. A moment's thought would have told my managers that the title was demeaning, that they would lose nothing and gain much by calling me an assistant sales manager and that there would be nothing artificial about this since it was an exact description of the job. Communication failures are often the result of such sloppy thinking.

Even though I earn my living communicating to others, it is continually impressed upon me how easy it is to fail because you've failed to adequately consider your listeners. Recently I was explaining a management technique to a group. It seemed to get across all right, and when I asked, "Do you understand the method, gentlemen?" there were confident nods around the room. I asked one of the group to recap the technique and he shrugged and said: "Well, Michael, I'm actually a little confused about it." Yet he had just indicated that he understood it!

Slightly shaken, I asked for a volunteer to explain it, and to my relief another member of the group came up to the board to rough out his idea of the subject I had just covered. Unfortunately he was completely off the track!

Only the week before I had run a similar management clinic for another group in the same company and had had no trouble at all. My immediate reaction was that this was a dim bunch, but that is too easy a trap to fall into. The fault was mine. It was my job as the communicator to discover the level of understanding of the listeners and to aim the training at that level, and this I had not done.

Frequent communication breakdowns occur when technical terms are used in speaking with nontechnical people or with people whose area of expertise is different than the one under discussion. Remember the sales director who had a problem with his distributors? You have technical terms in your industry too. Be careful when you talk about beta blockers, anticlines, COBOL, stratified charge, salt glazing, semiconductors, corona effects, or nematicides that you translate these into the language of the listener. It is a narrow path between insulting his intelligence by overexplaining, and bewildering him by not explaining, but the good communicator knows who his audience is and picks his words carefully.

KEEP IT SIMPLE

"All this is very well," you say. "But I have never been very good at English, and it's too late to start changing now. I can't very well learn the dictionary by heart."

To communicate well, you don't have to start learning long, impressive words and phrases. In fact it is much better if you don't. People who delight in four-syllable words have never been good communicators because they turn their listeners off. Here is a letter from my files, copied word for word. How does it grab you?

Dear Mr. Beer,

We are in receipt of your communication of the 13th instant, in which connection we beg to advise that the syllabus as laid out by your goodself is in concordance with our views.

Initially we were of the opinion that the seminar should bring more emphasis on the branch managers' responsibility specifications; however, we are now prepared to fall into line with your thinking on this matter.

The only suggestion we would like to bring forward at this stage is that the title of the seminar be: "The Branch Managers' Role in the Motivation Process."

Trusting that this will coincide with the parameters which you discussed telephonically with our Mr. ____, we remain,

Yours faithfully,

I keep this gem conveniently near me so that I can read it whenever I find that I am becoming pompous and verbose. Isn't it beautiful? There are 113 words in the body of that letter and most of them don't mean a thing. They could have written:

Dear Mr. Beer,

Thank you for your letter. Your syllabus seems quite satisfactory and we look forward to seeing you at the Eastern Hotel at 8:30 A.M. on March 27.

There are twenty-six words in that letter, and it gives me three pieces of information which the previous masterpiece did not, namely place, time, and date. The most amazing thing seems to happen to a perfectly normal man when he sits down to dictate letters. He suddenly seems to feel that he must use words more suitable to legal documents than to normal communication.

So don't worry if you haven't had the sort of education which produces an extensive vocabulary. You don't need it. If you can express yourself in simple terms, you can communicate well.

INITIATE ACTION

As the secretary said to her boss, "If you wanted me to do it right away why didn't you say so, instead of just marking it "Very Urgent?"

Many of the things you communicate are intended to cause someone to take action of some sort:

You want the service station to fix the ignition timing on your car but for god's sake not to replace the contact points because they did that last month and it didn't help.

You want your boss to rearrange the work schedule to avoid month-end bottlenecks.

You want your wife to stop getting bread from the supermarket because it tastes like damp cardboard, and get it from the Italian bakery even if it does cost twice as much.

You want your younger son to work out a fair ratio between playing the guitar and doing his homework.

Unless our communication results in the desired action, we can do a fine job of practicing the points made so far and still fail in communication.

We have to do a *selling* job in communication, and this is never more important than when we wish to get action started. You may not like the idea of "selling" people on the idea of taking action. You can't very well instruct your boss to get moving on something, but you can sure tell a mechanic what to do on your car without having to sell him on the idea! Certainly, but how you go about it can have a marked effect on how the job is done. If I had told my barber to quit using the blunt razor on me, he would have resented the implication that he was sloppy about maintenance of the tools of his trade, whereas by selling him on the sharpness of his razor I produced an attitude of pride and a painless haircut.

We sell the action by giving a *reason* for it. The best communication makes the reason a wanted result for the listener or, at least, the avoidance of an unwanted result:

If you are not charged for unnecessary contact points, there won't be a hassle about last month's bill.

If your boss rearranges the workload, everybody will get home on time at the end of the month and there will be less inter-departmental bickering.

If the family can get that Italian bread then there is a chance that Junior will actually eat his lunch instead of swapping his sandwiches for marbles.

If your son will donate equal time to the guitar and Napoleon's march on Moscow then he will be through with Napoleon in six months instead of having to meet him all over again next year.

Sell the idea of action. Where possible, watch the action being started (or better yet, help it to get started) and you stand a better chance of its being carried through to the end.

MEASURE THE RESULT

Communication is such a vital part of our lives that we should never stop trying to improve, to sharpen our skill at it. Try to develop the habit of rating yourself. Ask yourself: How did I do in that situation? Did I go about it in the right way? I goofed there—why? How do I do it next time?

I have formed the habit of secretly taping myself every now and then during training clinics I am running. I find this an invaluable and humbling exercise, because when I play it back in the privacy of my study I find glaring mistakes in my communication techniques. Only then do I notice that here I didn't talk the listener's language, there I brushed aside some participator's comment which could have led to fruitful discussion, and there I did not make sure that there was full understanding. All these goofs—and need I say once more that communicating is my *job,* that I make my living at it?

Come to think of it, you do too, don't you?

9

The Relatively Simple Art of Human Relations

When the subject of human relations comes up in a management clinic I usually see a few cynical smiles around the group. "Molly coddling" is a common reaction to any talk of human relations. Let us get this out of the way right now. Human relations is *not* molly coddling. It is not going around the workplace patting people on the head and asking them how their prize geraniums are getting on. If you are a Strong/Hard manager you will be tough, demanding, and remote—yet you can and should practice good human relations. All managers should, whether they are "hard" or "soft."

"Human relations" became a fad term between the wars, just as in more recent times job satisfaction, job enrichment, Management by Exception, and Management by Objectives have become the "in" terms. I don't knock these ideas. They all have their place in the scheme of things, although it is a little scary to see how managers receive each new theory with glad cries as the ultimate answer to all their problems. Each is merely an aid to good management, not a substitute for it. However.

THE COMPANY OUTING

With the rise of this new star called human relations, the Human Relations Consultants went around to managers of people and said, "It has been proved that if you practice good Human Relations, productivity goes up, staff turnover comes down, and morale is significantly improved." "Sounds great," said the managers. "What *is* Human Relations?"

"Well, you see," said the experts, "you start a company football team, you have an annual dinner and dance for the staff, you put suggestion boxes around the office and factory, you write a letter to each employee on his birthday, you scrap the executive diningroom and eat in the cafeteria with the peasants—all that sort of thing."

None of this looked particularly expensive, difficult, or dangerous, and many managers went ahead with it. They bought Ping Pong tables and started staff magazines and paid a visit to the shipping department (they had to ask where it was) and got soundly beaten at the company Putt-Putt tournament by a junior statistical clerk.

Then they sat back and complacently waited for all the wonderful things to come about which had been predicted by the experts. When absolutely nothing happened to productivity, turnover, or morale, they cursed, threw out the new ideas, and went back to the old feudal way of running things, and "human relations" fell into disrepute.

IT'S AN ATTITUDE

Now, in fact, those people you just read about were not practicing human relations. No doubt sports facilities and company outings are all to the good, but that is not what human relations is all about. Human relations is not a series of arrangements and technique. *It is an attitude of management towards staff*. You can't fake this attitude. You have to feel it and mean it, and unless you do, then anything you try on the purely cosmetic side of human relations will be a waste of time and money.

I am not, as my associates and family know, an expert on human relations, so I would rather leave the definition at that: it is an attitude of management towards staff. But let me give you some examples (both successes and failures) of human relations at work and see if we can come up with some practical guidelines. I hope to show that there is nothing mysterious about it, that it is one of the more simple arts of management, and that all that is required to practice it skillfully is a little common sense. That may sound a little arrogant since I am suggesting that we can do in one chapter what other people have taken 700-page books to do, but I believe that what we are discussing truly is a simple thing. Let's see.

TWO BLUNDERS

A company I worked for had its main branch office inland and a smaller branch office on the coast. The sales supervisor on the coast left us and we had to pick a successor. There was no question of promoting any of the coastal salesmen since none of them had the requisite experience or maturity, so we had to look for a candidate in the main branch. We found the very man. We called him in, gave him the good news, and for a while we had quite an emotional scene, with Miles proclaiming his gratitude to management, his awareness of the high honor bestowed on him and, with his hand on his heart, his love for and loyalty to the company. "Great, Miles," we said. "Dry your tears of joy and pack your bags."

"I can't accept the job," he said. "I would love to go and it breaks my heart to turn it down. But I have a little daughter who has asthma, and she can't live on the coast. Every time we take her there she chokes up; we have to live here. I have to turn the job down." We commiserated with him, assured him that we understood perfectly and that his future in the company was in no way jeopardized—and gave the job to Beasely, the next most suitable candidate.

And morale in that division of the company went down like a rock in a pond. The rumors started: "What has poor old Miles done to be passed over? He was the man for the job." "Just who do you have to know in this lousy company to be promoted?" "Beasely must be related to the top brass." Et cetera.

We never thought it necessary to get across to the team that Miles had not been passed over, because our attitude towards them had been wrong. Wrong? We didn't even *have* an attitude. We did try to repair some of the damage later by mentioning casually at a sales meeting that Miles had been offered the job but had decided to stay in the main branch because of family reasons. And then we nearly had another human relations problem on our hands because by saying that we implied that Beasely was very much a second choice (which of course he was), and we managed to ruffle his feathers as well.

Another example: A client of mine, an established drug company, has always been deeply concerned about its ethical approach to its customers and its employees and it has a fine reputation for excellent staff relations. In one part of the plant a group of girls packed an encapsulated drug into blister-packs. They worked in hygienic conditions, pay and fringe benefits were good, and morale was high. Then one girl left the company. A few days later another one gave notice. When the third girl came in to resign, the personnel manager realized that a pattern was forming, and the following dialog took place:

Personnel Manager: Suzy, you are one of our best girls. You have been with us for four years. Why are you leaving us? Is there anything we are doing wrong?

Suzy: No, I just feel I'd like a change, that's all.

Personnel Manager: Suzy, please. Tell me what the problem is. We don't want to lose you!

Suzy [*dissolving into tears*]: I don't *want* to go, but my husband says I have to leave before you fire me.

Personnel Manager: Now, why on earth should we fire you?

Suzy: Well, the company's going bankrupt, and you're going to fire everybody pretty soon.

Personnel Manager: Suzy, if the company was going broke I'd be leaving with you. We have just had our best year ever. Where did you get that crazy idea?

Then the whole story came out. The girls had noticed that fewer and fewer capsules were being processed, and they reasoned that since this was the company's main product that it was failing in the marketplace and that the company would soon start firing all the staff. Now, the facts were that the product was indeed being phased out of production, but this was to make room for a better product which promised to gain an even bigger share of the market.

Was Suzy stupid to view the situation as she did? Be careful before you judge her. Put yourself in her shoes, look at it from her perspective. All she saw was one simple, incontrovertible fact: the company was selling less product. From this she drew an erroneous *but completely logical* conclusion.

The real tragedy of poor human relations is that nine times out of ten, if management had only put both brain cells into gear and thought the situation through, the hassles need never have happened in the first place. And really, how difficult is that? You have some change of policy or procedure coming up which will affect your staff to a greater or lesser degree. How high does our IQ have to be in order to ask ourselves a few simple questions?

Exactly what is the situation?

Is it good news or bad news for the staff?

Never mind about that; will it seem to *them* like good news or bad news?

How best to get it across to them? Do we hold a staff meeting? If it will affect different people differently, should we tell them one at a time? How about a memo? Or do we tell their own supervisors first and get them to relay it?

Good human relations is indeed simple—all it takes is an attitude, a little grey matter, a little foresight and perception, a sensitivity to your people's point of view, and the ability to communicate.

NOW YOU'RE AN EXPERT

Well, now that you know what human relations is all about, here are three human Relations Problems which you should be able to handle standing on one leg. I have deliberately chosen a sales, an office, and a factory situation to make the point that these are *not* sales, office, or factory problems. They are *people* problems. Off you go, and don't peek. Work out your answers before you read on:

1. Cecil Padder is a good, steady salesman who has one little fault: he considers his expense account a second source of income, and his padding of expenses has reached the level of a fine art. Although it started in a small way it has now grown to between 5 and 10 percent of his expenses. What are you going to do?

    (a) Pull him in, go through his expense reports with him, show him that you know exactly what he is doing, and warn him that one more infraction means the cold dark world of outer space for him.

    (b) Let it ride. It's not a fortune and what the hell, good salesmen are hard to find.

    (c) Issue a general warning to the whole team that their expense accounts will be carefully watched for any padding.

    (d) Something else: _____

2. The office staff has been used to getting a small Christmas bonus every year for the past five years. This year money is tight and you can't really afford the bonus. Leonard Looselip, the office gossip, has spread the word that the golden eagle has no plans to land this year, and faces are long and sad. What are you going to do?

(a) Ignore the long faces and pay no bonus—they'll get over it.

(b) Call Leonard Looselip in and put the fear of God into him.

(c) Grit your teeth and pay the bonus—it won't kill you.

(d) Something else: _____

3. Yours is a marketing-oriented company, with the accent on sales, sales, sales. This is all very well, but it is having an adverse effect on your factory, where your production team under Thomas Grump seems to feel that it is the legion of forgotten men. Comments have filtered through to you that Sales are the golden boys, and that all Production gets is indifference when they do well and insults when they do badly. The factory work load usually does get done, however, although the percentage of waste and rejects is higher than you would like. What are you going to do?

(a) Nothing—there is no problem here. Production men always whine from time to time and the sky won't fall.

(b) Give the whole team 10 percent increase—you can afford it.

(c) Lean on Thomas Grump slightly. His job is to maintain morale and he isn't doing it.

(d) Something else: _____

There is something which links these three problems together, differing widely though they seem. I should love to hear your answers, but since I can't, here are some points:

1. CECIL PADDER

(a) Pull him in and threaten to fire him: Unless the crime is severe, most criminals get a stern warning for the first detected offence, with the clear indication that if there is another it means bad trouble. It may be a little harsh to apply (a) to Cecil if apart from this transgression his record is clean.

(b) Let it ride: I doubt you picked (b) unless you want a situation where the entire sales team if fiddling the expense account full time and selling only during coffee breaks.

(c) Issue a general warning: This looks like the obvious choice, but if you picked it you could be in trouble unless you worded your warning very, very carefully. Cecil will probably let it go right over his head (you haven't mentioned him by name so why should he worry?), while the innocent members of the group will resent being treated as crooks. Too dangerous, and ineffective anyway.

2. Leonard Looselip

(a) Don't pay: This is the simple solution and you would probably get away with it at the cost of temporarily lowered morale and a few resignations.

(b) Scold Leonard: Do this by all means if it relieves your feelings, but it won't help the problem. Leonard Looselip is a symptom of the disease, not the cause of it.

(c) Pay the bonus: Go ahead and pay if you feel you will lose less skin that way; it won't kill you. What about next year, though, if it turns out as bad as this year? And the year after that? Decisions, decisions.

3. Thomas Grump

(a) Ignore it: Nobody whines without a reason, and you know the reason in this case. To choose (a) is chickening out on a decision which you are going to have to make some time.

(b) Give Production a raise: Great idea, this, and the next time they are unhappy you just give them another 10 percent increase, and the next time. . . . You won't solve this problem by throwing money at it.

(c) Lean on Thomas? Why not? It certainly is his job to maintain group morale, and if the problem is of his making, either by omission or commission, then he should sort it out. Is it his problem, though? He only runs Production.

PREVENTING THOSE SITUATIONS
IN THE FIRST PLACE

Well, asking you to solve these problems was a little sneaky, because although I wrote them, I don't have the answers and neither does anyone else. No doubt you managed to produce some workable solutions, but that is not the point. The point—and the only point—is what links the three problems together. It is what is common to almost all people problems. Here it is. Carve it in marble:

> *It is a thousand times easier to* PREVENT *human relations problems from occurring than to* CORRECT *them when they have occurred.*

If we had stopped Cecil Padder dead in his tracks the very first time he had falsely claimed five cents for a parking meter, we would not have the present problem—which has now got out of hand. If years ago we had made it very clear that the bonus was not automatic but was linked to profits, if indeed we had had the sense to make it smaller one year and bigger the next, we would not have the present problem—which has not got out of hand. If we had realized that production people do tend to feel like Cinderellas and had done something about it long ago, we would not have had the the present problem—which has now got out of hand.

So, to eliminate human relations problems, foresee them. Set your standards right from the start. Look at things from the point of view of your people. Above all, tell them, *tell* them what is happening. Bring them as far as possible into management decisions, show them the big picture, ask their advice about changes. The examples are legion where management, stuck with an apparently insoluble problem, has consulted the man behind the lathe, the woman at the accounting machine, the man with the samples case—and has been rocked back on its heels when the logical, workable and obvious solution has come right back.

INVOLVE YOUR PEOPLE

Let us end with two situations which turned out well. I once had a secretary who had a rather boring but very responsible job. She had to type long, technically complex tenders for earthmoving machinery for submission to government agencies. One day I happened to have the complete clutch assembly of a class two crawler tractor on my office floor (every industrial sales manager's office looks like an unsuccessful scrapyard) and my secretary came in to take dictation.

"What on earth is that?" she asked, pointing at the clutch. "You've been typing that for about two years," I said. "That's the bimetallic clutch assembly we offer in our tenders as an optional extra."

"Oh, is *that* what it looks like!" she exclaimed. Why is it called *bimetallic?*" "Well, if you look at it closer—" I stopped. "Are you really interested?" "Of course I am!" she assured me.

The next week we began to send the office staff out to the factory in twos and threes. They spent most of a day there, looking at the assembly lines, having lunch at the canteen, riding the huge tractors, scrapers, and loaders out at the testing ground—and they had a ball.

We realized that we had something going here and we enlarged on the idea. Order clerks went into the field with salesmen and for the first time in their lives braved heat, cold, the irritation of looking for parking, and the wrath of customers. Salesmen donned greasy overalls and broke their fingernails stripping rustproofing off recalcitrant bulldozers. Accountants got their collars grimy fighting their way through piles of hydraulic hoses, doing stock counts in the parts department.

I don't pretend that all this had a dramatic effect on the attitude of the staff, but it certainly cut down on the amount of interdepartmental bickering and conflict. We had people come to us and say, "Hey, I never realized what a tough job those poor guys have!"

Tell your people, *show* your people, *involve* your people. And watch your human relations problems dwindle.

I sat in on what promised to be a really tough annual sales meeting of a client company. The company had had high hopes for a product which they had launched some months before and which had turned out to be a real lemon. (The best marketing organizations in the world do this from time to time—you can't win them all.) The product was as popular as a coffin at a christening, and the sales staff, bruised, battered, bloody, and low on morale, were sure they were going to be blamed for the failure.

The marketing director stood up to address the group. "Gentlemen, I deserve to be shot," he said. "Here I am, lucky enough to have one of the finest sales teams in the country and what do I do? I give you a product which is the wrong product at the wrong time in the wrong packaging with the wrong promotion and at the wrong price—and I expect you to sell it! I apoligize."

Well! The attitude in that conference room underwent such a rapid and profound change that you could literally feel it. And when one of the salesmen said, "Maybe *we* should have done better," there were murmurs of agreement from his colleagues. The director shook his head. "Thanks, fellows, but this goof was mine alone. Well, let's walk away from it. It's history, and we have all learned something from it. Now," he grinned at them. "Would you believe that with my obvious talent for picking lousy products, I have *another* new product for you?"

The group roared with laughter, and at that moment the new product was brought in and passed around. Now each man was keenly interested, and as the promotion strategy was explained to them it was obvious that they were right behind their manager and highly motivated to hit the market again.

That manager could have put the blame for failure on his salesmen, and he would have had a rebellious, truculent group who would have viewed the new product with jaundiced eyes and with the expectation of failure already built in. Instead he freely acknowledged that the fault was his and immediately brought them to his side. This was not pandering to them, it was not molly coddling them. It was the truth, and only the truth would have worked.

There is a hoary old saying that you can fool the people above you but you can't fool the people below you, and every manager could do worse than have this emblazoned on his office wall. That is what Human Relations is all about, and if I wrote a million words on it I could not say it any clearer.

Look at your attitude towards your staff and ask yourself, "Are my people working for me or against me?"

Hey—wouldn't it be fine if I could get them working *with* me!

10

The Stimulating Art of Incentives

This chapter deals with a sales management technique which can make the eyes of both manager and salesman gleam in anticipation. The manager dreams of sales figures skyrocketing and the salesman dreams of fat bonus awards and weekends in the Bahamas. Well, it can work out that way for management and for salesmen— or it can be a disaster of proportions beyond belief. The incentive scheme can be a powerful tool if properly handled, but unless it *is* properly handled it can lower morale, reduce sales instead of increasing them, and lead to resignations and firings at all levels.

We need to know exactly what we are talking about before we go into the details of incentives, and below is a breakdown of all the monies, fringe benefits, and other compensation a salesman can get from his job:

Remuneration	*Incentives*
Salary	Prizes and awards
Commission	from contests
Company car	
Pension fund	
Medical insurance	
Yearly bonus	

Now, it is stretching things a bit to describe health insurance as remuneration, but we do it to distinguish between two completely different concepts in what a salesman gets from his job. The column on the left describes those things which are *permanent*. If he has a contract with his company these are written into the contract. The column on the right, with only one item in it, describes something which is *temporary*. His company can have an incentive scheme this year, no scheme next year, three schemes the year after that, and so on. "But surely," you ask, "a salesman's commission is an incentive to sell more?" Quite right, it is, but that is not what we are examining in this section. We are looking only at temporary schemes and contests, used at the manager's discretion.

WHY INCENTIVES AT ALL?

A manager at a training clinic of mine once said, "If you have to buy extra business from your salesmen by paying them more to sell more, then something is wrong. Either you have done a bad marketing job, or your salesmen's targets are much too high, or you are not motivating them properly. An incentive scheme is simply a poor substitute for good management."

An interesting point, but this man did not recognize the fundamental idea behind incentive schemes. When you set up such a scheme you are not saying to your men, "You men have been dragging your feet, so in order to produce reasonable results I now have to pay you extra to get you to go out and do the job you should have been doing already." That isn't it at all. If you have that situation, then my manager was right and something is seriously wrong in your set up.

No, the real reason for incentives is this, and although you may not actually articulate it to your salesmen in quite this way, this is how they should see it: "You men have been doing a good job, and your sales figures are as high as anyone could reasonably expect. However, we need a higher volume for the next few weeks or months. If we are to reach this volume you will have to work harder. Now, if you do work harder and attain the figures we need, you have a right to expect something in return, and here it is. This is what we offer for getting the extra figures. You don't *have* to work harder, of course. There is nothing compulsory about this contest. All we are saying is that if you produce the *extra* effort and reach the targets you will get *extra* rewards." That's the feeling you have to get across.

There are many sales efforts which cannot be bettered with incentive schemes, and many others where such schemes should never be applied. Many of the opponents of incentives are against them because they have been involved in a scheme which was set up for the wrong reason or at the wrong time. If you have 92 percent of the market and your opposition is folding, it seems silly to add an incentive scheme for your salesmen. If you have a lot of back orders it is even more futile, yet I have seen money wasted in both these cases. Even more stupid is the use of a scheme to try to revive a product which because of more modern or superior opposition is dying a natural death.

When can incentives be useful? Here are some cases. You can probably think of others which suit your own marketing efforts:

If your products are seasonal, a contest can help to smooth out the dip in your sales graph.

If you have a product with good potential but which has simply not got off the ground, an incentive scheme can help promote that product.

If your opposition is about to launch a new product, you can foul up his impact on the market by filling up the stock shelves with your product.

If you are launching a new product, you can ensure bulk orders by awards for orders of certain sizes only.

If you need more dealer outlets, you can build the scheme around business done with new customers only.

Incentive schemes don't have to be run only for sales figures. I have seen excellent schemes where the targets were collection of monies owed, economy of operation, number of cold calls done and so on.

PLANNING THE SCHEME

So we intend to set up an incentive scheme. Let us say that in our company sales figures are level throughout the year (we are ignoring for the moment any seasonal fluctuations). Now, for reasons that seem good to us we wish to raise this level from April to July, so we institute an incentive scheme which will run for that time and we hope that our sales figures will climb upward for those months. We can also entertain the hope that the momentum engendered by the contest gives us some spin-off, and that sales will stay higher than normal for some time after the contest.

This would be great. It sometimes happens, though, to the astonishment and horror of the manager, that instead his sales actually drop well below the normal level in the month after the incentive scheme is terminated.

There are two reasons for a drop like this after the contest. Either your salesmen have done such a marvellous job of stuffing product into the pipeline that customers are full up for the moment, or (and this is only too likely) the entire sales force has sat back, put its feet up, and started a short, unofficial vacation.

Well, we can accept a small dip after the big rise if the rise has indeed been big enough, but what about the situation where there's a considerable drop *before* the contest and an immediate jump in sales figures the moment the contest begins? You know what has happened here, don't you? You have told your salesmen that you are setting up an incentive scheme next month, and their reaction to this has been to go around to their customers and say, "Thank you for the order. I am going to do you a favor. I'm dating it the first of next month, so you will have thirty days extra to pay it. Oh, not at all, don't thank me. It's a pleasure." Recognize one inescapable thing about your salesmen if you haven't yet: if there is a loophole in any scheme, instruction, policy, or procedure, then they will find it. The good Lord must love salesmen, he made so many of them, and I love them, too, but I know how their minds work and, believe me, that is how their minds work.

Luckily the solution to this problem is simple. Announce on Friday that the contest starts on Monday.

Most problems connected with incentives can be avoided by sitting down for a moment and thinking about them before hurling the contest at your men. Here are a few points:

1. What are we trying to achieve? There has to be a reason for the project—anything from assisting production planning to winning shelf space from your competitor. Let's make sure we know why we are doing it, and it better be a better reason than "Well, it's a year since we had our last one." That's no reason at all.

2. *What are the economics like?* A very useful thought for incentive schemes is this: Make friends with your cost accountant. Bring him into the whole deal and involve him very closely, or you may find yourself paying out more in prizes than you get back in increased sales. Your accountant, if he is worth anything at all, is the man who can show you that because of fixed costs, marginal costs, variable costs, breakeven points and all the rest of the costing mystique, you may be able, after reaching a certain sales volume, to pay out almost unbelievably handsome rewards and still be laughing. It could be a good idea to put your accountant on the panel or committee which runs the scheme. He will probably be so flattered (who ever invites accountants to anything at all?) that he will work very hard for you. Which leads us to our next point:

3. *Who should run it?* There is no reason at all why you should do all the work yourself and good reasons why you should not. First, there are specialists such as accountants to help you, and second, the scheme is much more likely to be accepted by the sales team if there are some peasants on the panel as well as the aristocrats. One of the most successful projects I was involved in had as the panel the marketing director, the chief order clerk, the accountant, the secretary to the production engineer, and the training manager (me).

4. *How long should it last?* This depends on what we are trying to achieve and, of course, how big the awards are. A full-blown, nationwide scheme can last six months or even a year, but a perfectly sound incentive is a supervisor saying to his team of three salesmen, "The man who sells the most in the next week is going on the town to a dinner and show with his wife, girlfriend or whoever." Too short a span and the thing never gets off the ground; too long and it drags—and this must never happen. The moment one man say, "Heavens, is that thing still going on?" you have a flop on your hands.

5. *What type of scheme is best?* This is perhaps the most important question of all. There are three basic types of incentive schemes, and each one has disadvantages as well as advantages.

INDIVIDUAL PRIZE SCHEME

The simplest, best-known, and easiest one to run is the individual prize scheme. There is a first prize for the winner, and maybe a second prize for the runner-up and a third prize and that's it. Nobody else gets anything. Hard luck, Bruno, and better luck next time.

Need it be emphasized that *never* should there be a booby prize? There are managers with the sort of mentality that reckons it is great fun, when the first and second prizes have been given out, to say, "Oh, yes, folks, we have one more prize. Bruno sold less than anyone else and we think it only right to award him a prize, too. At terrific expense we got this plastic donkey for you, Bruno. Come up and claim it!" I have actually witnessed this at the annual dinner-dance of the company concerned, and Bruno's wife was sitting next to him. Can you believe it?

What happens is that Bruno goes up and gets his booby prize, shakes the manager's hand, and says, "Thank you." That is what he is saying, but what he is thinking is, "Screw you, you bastard!" And he is on his way out of the company, looking for a boss who won't humiliate him.

You may say that the company could do without Bruno anyway, but the point is that this sort of performance has a very unhappy effect on the rest of the team. They fear that they could be in the same position next year, and morale drops all through the group.

As I said, the individual prize scheme is popular and much used. It is relatively easy to administer, the salesmen understand it because it is familiar, and the prizes can be worth winning since there are so few of them. The trouble with this type of contest—well, take a group of twenty salesmen. You announce the scheme, explain the prizes, and give them their individual targets. And right there and then, without moving from their seats, half of the group say, "I can't win. My territory is too small. My territory is too big. My opposition is too strong. My car is giving me trouble. I have this postnasal drip. No way can I win." They don't say all this to you, of course, but they are saying it to themselves. And right there you have lost half of your team from the contest.

So, ten of the twenty start to battle for the prize. About halfway through the contest it becomes obvious to everybody that only three or four men are in the running for top spot. What happens? The other six or seven give up the race, and you end with about 20 percent of the sales force still giving it all they've got, right up to the finishing line. That is one of the biggest disadvantages of the individual prize scheme—that it never involves everybody. There will always be dropouts. There is another problem, which is best expressed by a salesman: "It's not fair. I worked just as hard as Winston and he got the cup, the check, and the kudos, and all I got was a pat on the back." Resentment often follows the individual prize scheme.

TEAM PRIZE SCHEME

The second type of contest, and one which does away with some of the problems of the individual scheme, is the team prize contest. Here the sales force is split up into teams, either divisionally (the industrials, the consumer boys, the key accounts men, and so on) or geographically, where branches or districts compete against each other as teams.

This is a good scheme. There is little or no resentment, because the prize is divided among the team members and no single person wins. There is good team spirit going, too, with the stronger salesmen helping the weaker ones. Group pressure also works here, and if one man drags his feet, he is told very clearly by the rest of the group that he had better get moving unless he wants to practice driving his car with one arm in a sling.

Disadvantages of the team prize? The main one is that often the fine edge of the star salesman is blunted because his solo efforts are no so dramatically apparent. He is, he feels, harnessed to a bunch of cart-horses instead of winning the Grand National on his own.

POINTS SCHEME

The third scheme is the points system. It is my personal favorite, possibly because I have been involved with one or two highly successful points schemes. Here no salesman can lose because no salesman is fighting any other salesman; he is simply competing against his own individual target. There are no prizes as such at the end of the contest because each salesman is winning them throughout the period of the contest. As he hits his target figure each month he starts earning points (so many points for so much sold over his target).

These points can be traded for goods, and what usually happens is that the company gets a supply of catalogs from organizations specializing in this sort of thing (even a normal wholesaler's catalog will do very well) and awards points for the merchandise shown. Ten points and he can get a toaster, one hundred points and he can choose between a stereo set, a bicycle, or a dishwasher.

The advantages of the points system are many and attractive:

Interest in the scheme never lags. Indeed it increases as the months go by.

If someone is off sick for two weeks it doesn't put him out of the race; he can make a great comeback next month.

There is no resentment because nobody can beat anybody out of a prize.

Reward for effort is immediate; there is no waiting for months for the prizes.

Instead of only one incentive contest, there is the excitement of a new contest every month.

It lends itself to very good promotion by management so that interest is kept at a high level.

Of course, as the salesman collects his points, he can exchange them immediately for merchandise or he can save them up for a big prize from the catalog. We once sent the catalogs to the wives of the salesmen with an explanatory letter, so that when Ackroyd came home Mrs. Ackroyd had her feet up and was paging through all the wonderful things he was going to win for her! It worked, too.

Disadvantages of the points system? Mainly the administration of the scheme, since it is more complex than a simple prize scheme. Unless the promotion of the scheme is good, there may be a certain loss of competitive spirit because of there being no big winner, although you can have an overall prize at the end for the man who is furthest over his target.

SETTING QUOTAS

Having picked the type of contest which suits us best, we are now faced with the hardest part of incentive schemes. We have been stalling long enough and we now have to grit our teeth and get down to it. I am talking about setting the individual targets, and if we goof on this then goodbye contest.

What follows is so important it almost deserves a chapter on its own. It goes well beyond incentive contests. Whether you have incentives or not, you are still faced with the problem of setting quotas or forecasts or budgets or targets for each salesman for his working year, and we may as well look at this headache here as anywhere else.

I have been calling them targets, but to be picky they should really be called quotas. Strictly speaking there are three figures which apply to a salesman's figures for the year. There is the *target*, which is the highest of the three and which is that volume of sales which we would *like* him to reach. Then there is his *quota,* which is the figure we think he *should* be able to reach. Finally there is his *budget,* and this one is the figure he damn *has* to reach to make sure that we are not actually losing money on him. So let us call them quotas, just to have a word.

Probably the best way to describe the business of setting quotas is to do it through examples. We have this company which sells retrorefractive truncates, and because we are not stupid our salesmen have individual territories and individual quotas. I do sometimes find marketing organizations which do not give their salesmen individual quotas. The reasoning behind this remains a mystery to me. If you don't give your man something to reach for, how do you ever know whether or not he is reaching?

For the first problem in quota setting we assume an impossible hypothesis: that there is such a thing as two identical sales territories. There can be no such phenomenon, but we need to imagine it to identify the problem. Call them territories A and B. These territories are identical in every way except one, that the total potential for retrorefractive truncates in territory A is twice that in territory B. Thus:

Territory:	A	B
Total Potential:	100,000 units	50,000 units

If we are looking for a 25 percent share of the retrorefractive truncate market, then quotas will be allotted as follows:

Territory:	A	B
Total Potential:	100,000 units	50,000 units
Quota:	25,000 units	12,500 units

Fairly elementary so far. But now we want extra effort, so we allot awards for extra sales. We do realize, don't we, that it is twice as difficult for the salesman in territory B to sell 1,000 truncates over his quota as it would be for salesman A? So any increase in B is worth twice as much as a similar increase in A; one truncate sold in B is worth two sold in A. Therefore any award system can work only on a *percentage* increase, not on a *unit* increase.

For some reason this simple fact is hard for some managers to understand and accept. They will insist on looking at absolute increases over quota when the least bit of intelligent thought would show them that this is meaningless. Percentage increase is the only possible way to compare the selling efforts of your men.

For the next problem we assume two completely identical territories, with identical potentials. In A we have Alfred, a mature, experienced man who has been in this territory for ten years. Alfred knows his territory and his customers well and is our most senior salesman. In territory B we have little Morris. We hired Morris three months ago, slammed him through a condensed product knowledge course, pointed him in the general direction of his customers, and wished him luck. Now, figuring again on a 25 percent share of the truncate market. Alfred gets a quota of 25,000 units:

Territory:	A	B
Salesman:	Alfred	Morris
Total Potential:	100,000 units	100,000 units
Quota:	25,000 units	?

Big question. What quota do we give Morris? Well, surely it is only fair to start him with a lower quota than Alfred, say 12,000 or

15,000 units, since he has to find his footing in his new territory and he does not have the knowledge or experience which Alfred enjoys. Let's say 15,000 units for Morris, right?

Wrong.

Quotas are given to a *territory,* not to a *salesman.* They are not based on experience, *they are based on potential of the territory.* "But what about Morris?" we ask. "He won't stand a chance in the contest if he has the same quota as Alfred. What are we trying to do, break his spirit before he gets off the ground?"

Good point, and we may have to award a small special prize for effort or for most improved figures or something like that for which Morris would be able to strive. But in this situation our real consideration must be Alfred. Suppose we do give Morris an easier quota than Alfred, and here we are sitting in our office the day after we have announced those quotas. Alfred walks in. "What the hell is this," he barks, "A kindergarten? What are you doing giving the new guys easy quotas and hitting me with a tough one? Doesn't my hard work over the years to bring my territory up mean anything at all?"

Well, you gave Morris the easier quota, so you answer Alfred while I hide behind the filing cabinet. Quotas are based on potential of the territory, not on potential of the salesman.

Another one—identical potential for A and B:

Territory:	A	B
Total Potential:	100,000 units	100,000 units
Salesman:	Alfred	Humbert
Last Year's Sales:	25,000 units	15,000 units
This Year's Quota:	28,000 units	?

In this case both Alfred and Humbert have been in their territories for ten years. Both are experienced salesmen. The territories are identical in every respect. Now, because of good and sufficient reasons we believe that we can grab another 3 percent of the total market. We have a big promotion coming up and we are putting a new line of retrorefractive oblates into the market to back up our truncates. So, we give Alfred another 3,000 units and his total quota for this year is now 28,000.

Big question: What do we give Humbert? Well, surely we add 3,000 units to his last year's sales, same as we did for Alfred, and that gives Humbert a quota of 18,000 units. That's only fair, right?

Wrong.

Consider our hypothesis. The territories are identical *in every respect.* (Impossible in real life but it makes the point.) Even if we did fall into the trap of giving the quota to the salesman instead of to the territory, both Alfred and Humbert are equally experienced. Therefore, Humbert is either not as good at selling as Alfred or, more likely, he has simply been coasting along while Alfred has been working hard. So we give Humbert a lower quota for the contest, and by doing a halfway decent job of work this year he wins it? No way. He gets 28,000 (or his territory does), same as Alfred's territory, and if he doesn't like it, well, things are tough all over, Humbert, and I suppose that we can stumble along without you—we're certainly going to try.

Well, those are some of the problems which make the setting of quotas such a headache. It will not have escaped you that I have given no magic formula for estimating total potentials in territories, and this is no oversight. I simply can't do it. Done properly, this can be a complex and highly expensive business, involving market research, population growth, shifts in the economy, demographic surveys, socio-economic trends, and all the other impressive-sounding ways of finding out just how many people or companies are in a position to buy how much of the product you sell.

Most managers get their figures by working on past sales in the territory (and we have seen in Humbert's case how dangerous this can be), coupling this with what head office *wants* this year and the heck with what you think you can *get,* mate. This is possibly reinforced by throwing knuckle bones in a circle of brimstone by the light of the full moon. It may sound cynical, but both this way and the most expensive market research may be equally out of line. Thank the gods that it is no longer my job.

We seem to have spent a lot of time on quota setting, but there is one more aspect of it which we must mention, and it goes like this: You as the sales manager have estimated a total sales figure for your team. In effect this is *your personal quota,* since you are responsible for overall sales. Let us say that this figure is 7 percent higher than last year. You now have the job of splitting this total figure into chunks and of giving each man a chunk. Remember that your figure is increased by 7 percent. Will you tell me then why you insist on increasing each salesman's quota by 10 percent? All right, perhaps you don't do this, but a lot of managers do, and they are headed on a collision course with their sales team. The reason they give for loading their men with the extra 3 percent is that they will strive that little bit harder and at least make the 7 percent which was all that was required in the first place.

All very well, but do you recall the fable of the boy who cried wolf? You can do it once maybe, but never again, and in the meantime you will have lost the confidence and trust of your men. They will never believe when you hand out quotas in future that you aren't loading them again, and they will do their own discounting of your figures.

THE PRIZES

Make sure that all the prizes for your incentive scheme are acceptable to all the contestants. It is useless to award a camera as a prize if half of your team is not in the least interested in photography and the other half already has better cameras than the one you offer. Gift certificates are a safe way, but somehow it is difficult to get turned on by a gift certificate, no matter how generous it is, and you can't frame it and hang it on the wall for your friends to admire.

Money is always acceptable, and many companies simply write out a check and hand it over. But remember that any prize won in an incentive contest is taxable income in most countries in the world (better check yours), and if the winning salesman is already a successful man then his income is probably already taking a savage beating from the taxman. Your salesman has certainly taken this into account in deciding whether it is worthwhile doing a real job in the contest or not.

It is often a source of astonishment to many managers that a salesman who wouldn't cross the street for the chance of winning a cash prize will often sweat and strain, body all achin' and racked with pain, in order to win a silver cup with his name on it. For this man the real joy of winning is the acclaim of his peers. (It never worked that way with me—just spell my name right on the check.)

Even if the prize is cash, it does make sense to give a cup or a shield with it. The cost is negligible, and electroplate looks just like silver from five feet away.

LAUNCHING THE SCHEME

The launch of the scheme sets the tone, and it must be done right. If feasible it is best to do it with a meeting rather than sending a memo to each man. A meeting allows questions and comments, and you can induce a feeling of dynamism about the contest. Keep the rules as simple as possible, and make sure that every contestant understands them. Allow plenty of time for questions, but, as in all meetings, the questions should be of a general-interest nature. Any individual problem should be handled outside the meeting.

Make sure that the group accepts the quotas as fair and realistic—or agrees that they are as fair as humanly possible. No incentive scheme in the world can ever be entirely fair to all participants because no one can foresee all circumstances. For example, the sales manager of a tractor company can set seemingly equitable quotas for his men, but if halfway through the contest a good rain in one territory allows farmers to get on with the plowing, then that salesman is going to sell more tractors than salesmen whose prospective customers are gloomily staring at lands where the wind is taking off their topsoil. There is nothing you can do about this kind of situation. Certainly you cannot change quotas halfway through the contest. Salesmen are not stupid, and they will generally accept figures which are based on the best information available at the time, as long as they are informed of why, how, and who.

It is a good idea to build the contest around a theme of some sort. To give you an idea of how far back I go in this sort of thing, the first incentive scheme I was ever involved in was around the time that Hilary and Tensing were fighting their way up Mount Everest. We called the contest "First Man up the Mountain," and corny as it was, it was topical and it worked well. Build your scheme around a horse race if you like, and make each salesman a horse. Most of the salesmen I have worked with believe that they work like horses anyway, and this may appeal to them. We did this once and in addition we made the office staff the jockeys. Each jockey had a salesman horse, and the jockeys received small prizes if their horses did well. This did no harm and it made the internal staff feel involved.

Once the contest is under way, don't let the impetus die. Keep interest high with progress letters, telegrams to those men who have done particularly well during a week, bulletin boards in the sales office with the names of the latest leaders, that sort of thing. If the scheme is big enough, it makes sense to get some special letterheads for all mail and announcements, and do it right;—get a professional to do the artwork instead of letting your sister's little boy loose on it because "he was always good at drawing."

HOW ABOUT INVOLVING THE SPOUSE?

There is the thorny problem of how far to go in bringing the salesman's wife into the contest. On the one hand it can work well, with the wife encouraging him, helping him with his paperwork, and on occasion even doing some telephoning for appointments. On the other hand—well, I thought I was being very clever once when I sent out a weekly letter to the wives of a group of my salesmen who were in an incentive scheme. It was, I thought, a harmless, chatty little note telling them how the contest was going. But I got a very stiff letter back from one woman who made it clear that while the company might think that it owned Porteus body and soul during working hours, after hours Porteus belonged to her, and would I please keep office business out of her home. Can't win them all.

What is worth considering, and has worked wonderfully well, is sending each wife a bowl of flowers at the end of the contest, especially if her husband was not in the winner's circle. Include a note saying that while Porteus didn't win, he tried hard and that you appreciate that she must have missed out on Porteus's company while he was working late—you know the sort of thing to say. This has always had a good reaction, and the letters we have received in response have been very positive.

Here's a few more points. Get the boss to dig into his expense account and donate a couple of mugs of beer to the halfway leader. Give a special prize to the man who manages, in the hurly-burly of the race, to keep his outstanding debtors down. Put up the photographs of the leaders each week in the reception area, and so on and so on. Never under any circumstances whatever mention the names of the losers in a disparaging tone, either by written memos or by speech. They get the message well enough simply by not being mentioned, and they are smarting enough because of their failure without your rubbing salt into it.

WHEN THINGS GO WRONG

I once had a manager in a clinic who was unalterably opposed towards incentive schemes. His company had tried them and they caused more resentment, low morale, and poor sales figures than anything they had ever done. It was only when chatting with this man during lunch that I learned the truth, and then it all came clear to me. It turned out that they had tried only one incentive scheme, and halfway through the contest they had realized that they had set their quotas too low, and their salesmen were cashing in and winning the prizes too easily. You may not believe this, but the management then and there, halfway through the contest, *changed the rules*. They announced a 20 percent increase in quotas and reduced the prizes—and wondered why on earth their sales force went into hibernation for the rest of the contest.

If you ever find that you have goofed by making the contest too easy, then the solution is also easy: you bite the bullet, smile through your tears, and leave it as it is.

Oddly enough, a time may come in an incentive scheme where you may find it necessary to do the reverse. We started a contest which was headed for success. We got the quotas dead right, the salesman liked the prizes, and the results for the company looked good. Suddenly our supplier overseas was hit by a series of strikes and supplies became erratic. It was heartbreaking to see a salesman bring in a really juicy order and have to tell him that because of slow shipments we simply could not honor it. In this case we called a meeting and explained the position. Have I said it before? I'll say it again: Salesmen aren't stupid, and the team appreciated our frankness and the impossibility of continuing the contest with the same format. Nevertheless, they had worked hard, and we arranged a modified scheme *with their approval* which did not hit the company too hard and yet gave them something for their efforts. Morale was kept high and selling effort was maintained.

Done right, incentive schemes can be a powerful tool in the management of salesmen. Almost all the arguments against incentives are from managers who have had the misfortune to be involved in a scheme which was ineptly run or which should never have been run. But abuse of a thing has never been an argument against it, and it would be a pity to be scared off something which can do so much good.

11

The Entertaining Art of Running Sales Meetings

This chapter is not a how-to on public speaking. I don't know too much about public speaking, although I have made quite a reasonable living at it. What it *is* about is the art of running your regular sales meetings. It is still a source of astonishment to me that many managers actually fear sales meetings. This is a pity, because your sales meetings can and should be fun things. You and your salesmen should *enjoy* them.

A NOTE ON PUBLIC SPEAKING

I said that this chapter is not a child's guide to public speaking, but perhaps we should spend a moment on the subject because there are many excellent managers who do an outstanding job in every other aspect of management. But when they have to stand up and talk at a sales meeting they act as though they have simultaneously been struck with laryngitis, amnesia, and St. Vitus' dance. Why? They are talking to people who are by no means strangers, who are in subordinate positions to themselves, and who have not even paid to get in. They are talking about things which are familiar to them and about which they know more than their audiences. So what is the problem?

Whatever the problem, taking a course on public speaking may not be the answer. I once agreed to make an address at a public speaking course being sponsored by an association whose work for charity I much admired. Since I had an hour to kill, I sat at the back of the room and listened to part of the first lecture. It blew my mind.

According to the speaker, to be a success at this public speaking bit, you must dress correctly ("Err on the formal side," he said), stand with your toes pointing out (I'm not kidding, that's what the man said), have your notes typed on a special typewriter which types big, avoid familiar words and phrases (don't ask me why, he didn't say), and so on.

I left the meeting realizing what trouble I was in. I err on the sloppy side, I don't use any notes, I usually sit on the speaker's table, I swing my legs while I'm talking, and since I don't look at my feet during this exercise I have no idea where my toes are pointing. I'm not sneering at this lecturer. Maybe these things are important sometimes. But I do not believe that which way your toes point has anything to do with whether or not you are running a good meeting.

There is a secret to public speaking, and we will look at it at the end of the chapter. At the moment we are interested in the content of your meetings, not whether you come across like Cicero.

WHY MEETINGS FAIL

Sales meetings must be looked at with one thought in mind, and everything we say here hinges on this thought:

> *When salesmen come out of a meeting they must feel better than when they went into it, not worse.*

And how many sales meetings conform to that creed? Why do our salesmen so often leave a meeting feeling worse than when they went in, lower in morale and enthusiasm, when the whole purpose of the meeting was to raise these, not dash them to the ground?

There are many reasons for the failure of a sales meeting, but the most common is very simple: Many sales meetings fail because they are not *sales* meetings. You have sat through many meetings where the agenda has turned into a boring iteration and reiteration of administrative trivia, where ten men sit in a near-comatose state while the manager argues with Benson about his slow-paying customers.

That's not a *sales* meeting!

Nobody will argue that when you get your salesmen together you usually have to get some administrative information or instruction across to them. But what happens is that this part of the meeting drags on and eventually takes over the sales part, and it becomes a tedious, dragging affair when it should be turned-on and exciting.

A sales meeting exciting? Certainly! Why not? You have a choice: Your salesman can say, "Oh, no, not another of those dreary sales meetings!" Or they can say, "I wonder what the boss has laid on for the sales meeting?" Which attitude would you prefer?

Have a set time for the administrative part of the meeting and never allow it to encroach on the sales part. Stop in the middle of a sentence if necessary. Also, try to make even the administrative part general rather than individual, if you have to lean on Charlie about his complaint action reports, then do it outside the meeting; otherwise you are wasting the time of the rest of your crew. (In any case, pulling one man up for a misdemeanour in front of his peers is bad practice.)

WHEN AND HOW OFTEN TO MEET

How often should we hold sales meetings? I don't know. Once a week, once a fortnight, once a month—it depends to some extent on the logistics. If you have a sales force which is spread around the country, it simply does not make sense to drag them away from their territories too often. Good meetings can be anything from a two-hour affair held once a week to a whole day once a month, whichever best fits your scheme of things.

When should we hold meetings? This is a controversial subject. Friday afternoon? But then they go home for the weekend and forget all they have learned by Monday morning. Saturday morning? But who likes to come in on a Saturday morning? Monday morning? But that cuts into their selling week. There is an objection to any time you choose, but my own favorite is Saturday morning once a month. No one can object to one morning a month, no selling time is lost, the whole morning can be used to make the meeting worthwhile, and even the out-of-town salesmen can come in late on Friday night and have one night only away from base.

There may be a good reason for you to pick a different time. I have no deep-rooted views on this except to say that I don't very much like Monday morning. It is true that you can fire them with zeal for the coming week, but it really does cut into prime selling time. I have an unhappy feeling that when the group leaves the conference room it moves in a body to the nearest coffee shop and continues the meeting—or rather the discussion of Saturday's big game.

TEN WAYS TO BREAK THE PACE

A golden rule for instilling some life into your meetings is this: Break the pace. Get away from the routine and go a little far out if necessary, but break the pace in some way or other. Here are ten ideas to help you turn your meetings into something which your men will come out of feeling better than when they went in instead of worse. They are all designed to produce two things about the meetings: *novelty* and *involvement*. No doubt you are already using some of these, but the others may give you a series of subjects around which you can build your next few meetings.

PRODUCT ANALYSIS

Take one product from your range. Give each member of the team one feature of the product on which he will talk for exactly three minutes. Tell them in advance of the meeting, so that the talks can be prepared. When everyone has given his talk, have an open discussion around the group. There is a belief that salesmen of such products as toothpaste, tea bags, tobacco, or toenail clippers need not go deeply into product analysis because the buyer of a chain store is not interested in the components of the product. This may be true, but in their case product analysis means display, point-of-sale promotions, packaging, special deals, shelf pressure and so on, and a fruitful, high-participation meeting can be held around these things.

FILMS

While films were not created specifically for your own particular sales situation, they can be used as a basis for discussion in a sales meeting. Rent one or two from the many companies which specialize in business films and explain to the group before you show the film that they will be asked to comment on the techniques illustrated and to adapt them to their own products. The point is that merely to show the film has little effect unless there is discussion afterwards.

QUIZZES

With no prior warning, hand out a product knowledge quiz of, say, twenty questions. Set a time limit and get the group to swap papers for marking. Give a prize to the winner. The questions should be of the sort which can be answered briefly and factually instead of requiring an opinion, so that there can be no argument about the correctness of the answers. The rest of the meeting can be a discussion on those questions to which most of the group gave wrong answers.

KNOW YOUR ENEMY

Run this meeting in the same way as the product analysis one, except that a competitive product is the subject. If at all possible, have an actual product at the meeting. This is often easier than it sounds. Even if you sell front-end loading shovels, one can often be borrowed from a contractor. If this is not possible, it makes a break in your usual meetings to take the group to where the competitive model is operating. Printing machinery, for instance, can be seen at work in the shop of a friendly printer. In any case, have photographs, opposition literature and brochures, and comparative specification sheets available. The important thing here is to be completely honest and open about the good points of the opposition. Don't ever try to hide from your men that they are fighting good products.

ROLE PLAYING

Role playing can be a powerful sales meeting technique if properly done. It is a face-to-face enactment of a customer-salesman interview, with one salesman taking the part of the customer and another being himself. Pick your two "actors" carefully for this. A couple of noisy extroverts can easily turn the meeting into a farce, whereas the shy, withdrawn types can go into catatonic shock at being thrust into the limelight. Allow them to rehearse beforehand if they wish. This is a good time to use a tape recorder because you can stop the action during playback and ask for analysis and comments from the group.

Role playing is not universally popular because of its limitations, the main one being that it is an artificial situation and the group knows this. Also, it does not show how well the actors will perform in the field. Nevertheless, there are sound reasons for using this meeting technique. It is one of the very best ways to practice the handling of sales resistance, especially if the "customer" is encouraged to throw objections at the "salesman."

Role playing also very quickly shows any lack of product knowledge, not only in the actors but also in the group when they make their comments afterwards. It is a high-participation meeting, which is always a healthy thing. Lastly, if it is well done, then the salesmen seem to enjoy it—which by itself is reason enough for doing it.

SKITS

This is different from role playing in that a skit is an actual "play" written by you and enacted by two members of your group. It is not usually necessary for them to learn it by heart as they can very well read it from your script. The point here is that there are usually two scripts, the first one having all the wrong things a salesman can say and do in a sales interview, and the second script where these things are corrected. Stop the action after the first skit (it could very well be on tape) and ask for comments. Then play the second skit. This is something of a nuisance to prepare, but the effort is well worth while.

BRAG SESSION

Get one of your men who has done exceptionally well in gaining a big order, beating the opposition, or opening an important account to stand up and tell the group how he did it. This can be an astonishingly good meeting, because first, the salesman likes bragging a little and second, the other salesmen get the idea that it would be a nice thing to be able to stand up there and do some bragging of their own.

GRIPE SESSION

If properly handled, this meeting can help significantly in reducing gripes about other departments. Here we invite the production manager, technical engineer, or similar official to the meeting, and let your salesmen loose on him. As long as there is good will on both sides (and providing your technical man is big enough to take it) this can be an unbelievably effective meeting.

The session must be kept general. We don't want someone spending twenty minutes complaining about that one shipment that went wrong. But in this meeting we have a chance for the salesmen to express their viewpoint and then to hear from the horse's mouth why it is so expensive to stop an entire production line so that one customer can have two yellow stars on his order instead of the three blue rings which are standard.

Money Session

It may not sound very exciting, but I have attended some truly excellent meetings where the financial manager or comptroller is invited to explain the economics of marketing—where the money comes from, where it goes, the importance of profitability, what cash flow means, why poor cash flow is so expensive to a company, and so on. If the speaker gets his subject across well and is prepared to answer questions from the floor, your salesmen will show more interest than you may think possible.

Bring a Customer

If you want to blow your salesmen's minds, get a customer (and for heaven's sake pick him very, very carefully) to sit in on a meeting—and give him carte blanche to say exactly what he thinks about salesmen. I recently sat in on such a meeting and set with my mouth open the whole time. We were lucky because the man we invited was basically friendly towards the company and his attitude towards its products was good. But this did not stop him from hitting very hard. He started by saying, "Do you know why buyers are such bastards? In most cases, they catch the disease from the salesmen who call on them."

This customer was quite happy to answer questions, and it turned into one of the most profitable sales meetings I have ever attended. The company gave him a small gift and we had a few drinks afterwards. It was a great meeting, and it gave us enough to talk about so that we could actually use the points brought up to build the next sales meeting.

These ten ideas have worked for other managers and they can work for you. The success of your meetings is limited only by your imagination.

Remember that people do not develop when you talk to them; they develop when they talk to each other. Use every technique you can to get good, provocative participation in your meetings. Get away as far as you can from the "schoolmaster" atmosphere. When the people who are attending one of my clinics get so involved in talking to each other about the subject at hand that I could get up and walk out of the room without their even noticing, then I know I am really running a successful meeting.

And that goes for you, too.

THE SECRET OF PUBLIC SPEAKING

I promised that I would give you the secret of good public speaking. Well, here it is, the Magic Formula, for whatever it's worth. You have no doubt sat at the feet of speakers who were so good that they could talk sailors out of a strip-tease show, and you have wondered how you could ever emulate their oratory. Don't even try. The best tip you will ever get on being a good public speaker is:

> *Be yourself. Don't ever try to copy a speaker you happen to admire, because you are not that man and you never will be. Be yourself.*

Some magic formula, eh? That may be disappointing advice, but, believe me, that's your magic formula. The Italians have a saying: "We were born originals. Let us not die copies." Good advice. And here's another piece of advice:

> *Stand up and talk to a group just as though you were talking to one man, and you will be amazed at how you come across.*

I learned that secret from a man who was a business partner of mine for several years. I always envied his talent for getting any group on his side the moment he started speaking, and it was some time before I realized that his secret was a very simple one: no matter what size the audience was, he talked exactly as though he was talking to one man, and at no time did he ever try to copy another style of speaking. He was himself at all times.

Talk to the group, whether it is ten people or two hundred, as though you are talking to one man. You will find that it is easy to be yourself, and an original you will be much better at running a meeting than a copy of someone else.

12

The Dreadful Art of Appraisal

I spend a lot of time talking to managers, and when managers get together they seem to talk about the people who work for them. Often, a manager will say something like this to me:

"Do you remember old Benton from my team? He came to one of your training clinics." I acknowledge that I remember Benton.

"You know, we had to fire him," says the manager. "He was never any damn good."

At this point I should either murmur condolences in the manner of someone sympathizing about the death of a not-much-loved aunt or keep my mouth shut. But I usually say something like, "So Benton was never any damn good? Tell me, did you also fire the manager who hired Benton in the first place? He was no damn good at selecting his men!"

Of course, this is hardly the way to make friends, and the reaction of the manager is usually: "Now, hang on, Michael. It isn't as simple as that. When we hired Benton he was okay. He did a perfectly competent job for us for a couple of years, no problems at all. Then for some reason he simply began to go downhill until he wasn't cutting it any more and we had to fire him."

Now here is where I certainly should shut up, and I usually do so unless my death-wish is particularly dominant at the time. But what I feel like saying is, "So Benton just slowly went downhill, did he? Tell me, where was Benton's manager at the time? What was he doing while Benton was busy going downhill? Teeing up for the dogleg thirteenth?"

This is unfair. There are many reasons for a man's performance becoming substandard, and many of them have nothing to do with his manager, nor can the manager do anything about them. Ill health, domestic problems, money problems—these are common reasons for a man's work to suffer and none of them within the manager's ability to rectify.

Nevertheless there are also many things which the manager can do something about, and the time to do it is not when Benton has gone so far down the hill that he is no longer retrievable. The time to do it is when he first starts to show a deterioration in any aspect of his work.

And there is only one way in the whole wide world to discover this deterioration. That is by a formal system of appraisal or evaluation.

AN OBJECT OF NEGLECT

Staff appraisal is probably the most neglected, most underrated, and most feared of all management skills. I was discussing company policies and procedures with a manager before running a series of training clinics for his staff, and I asked whether the company used any type of appraisal system. Sure, I was told, they had installed a system some years ago. I asked to see a copy of the appraisal form and the manager called his secretary in.

"Lulu," he said, "get Mr. Beer a copy of our appraisal form, will you?"

Lulu looked blank. "Our what?"

The manager acted a little irritated. "Our appraisal form. You know, that blue sheet."

Lulu looked blanker. "I've never seen anything like that," she declared. "But I've only been here for eighteen months. Maybe Suzy knows about it."

Suzy vaguely recalled seeing something like that around some-where, and they eventually tracked down a pile of the forms under some cartons at the back of the stockroom. They had the *forms,* but they had stopped using the system.

If your company is not actively using an appraisal system at this moment, then five will get you ten that somewhere in your offices there is a stack of forms, dusty, dogeared, discolored and disused.

Sometime in the past someone, full of hope and high endeavor, instituted an appraisal system. It is no more. Why?

A formal performance appraisal system is the best way in the world to keep a worker up to the standards of his job specification. It is the best way to show him how to get back up there when he slips from the standards. It is a wonderful way of welding the manager and the man into an effective working team. It is by itself a powerful way of producing self-motivation.

If it is all these things, why do managers not grab it and use it eagerly? Why, why, why? The answer is simple and tragic. Managers reject this wonderful technique *because it frightens them out of their wits*.

THE DANGERS OF APPRAISAL

In the chapter on motivation we discussed the simple truth that we like to do those things we do well. The opposite is equally true—we dislike and fear doing the things we do not do well. Most managers fear the appraisal system because they don't know how to do it. They have never been taught it, and if they have ever tried it they have probably fallen on their noses, because it is another one of those skills which is not natural to most of us. We have to acquire it.

The trouble is that appraisal is such a *public* sort of thing. If you try to draw a self-portrait and fail miserably, nobody need know about it but you. You tear it up and walk away from it. If you try to evaluate an employee and go through the whole bit of filling in the form, running the appraisal interview, and then reporting to your boss, then at least two other people know how inept you have been—the man under you as well as the man above you. Too dangerous. Much better not to start it in the first place.

I completely failed to sell one management group on the idea of staff appraisal. The harder I tried to show them the advantages, the more they turned their faces against it. One said, "No way am I going to sit opposite one of my men and show him that I am marking him on a piece of paper. He will think that I'm treating him like a schoolboy, and I've got too much respect for my men to do that." Another said, "It is hard enough to get good people to work for you without chasing them away from the company with this sort of witch-hunt."

The most interesting reason came from the most perceptive man in the group. He smiled at me and said, "No. I can see that it could do everything you claim for it, but still no. Every time I did an appraisal on one of my men *I would also be appraising myself.*"

And right there, he hit the nail on the head. When you evaluate the performance of one of your staff you also evaluate your own. You are saying loud and clear, "This is how he is doing his job, and since I am his manager it is an indication of how I am doing mine." Hell no, that *is* too dangerous. That would make me too vulnerable to criticism, and I get enough criticism without my asking for it. Let's just forget the appraisal idea. Lots and lots of companies seem to do pretty well without it.

THE REWARDS OF APPRAISAL

Maybe some companies do get on well without an appraisal system. But in my experience the companies who use one are also those companies where there is a truly great spirit between boss and worker, where men and women know precisely what is expected of them, where standards are maintained and targets are reached, and where staff turnover is low and morale is high. Think *that* over a bit.

Naturally we fear staff evaluation if we do it badly, because the consequences of doing it badly are potentially disastrous. The consequences of doing many things are potentially disastrous, from hang-gliding to fire-eating, but that doesn't stop people from doing these things. They simply make sure that they do them well. They prepare themselves properly and they know exactly what to do.

Staff appraisal is not really all that difficult or frightening. It does not take very much time, since it is usually done not more often than twice a year. The form itself is simple to understand and fill in. The appraisal interview is relatively brief, and it should be pleasant and positive in atmosphere, not recriminatory. So simple—and the rewards in terms of staff satisfaction, productivity, and good human relations are rich.

YOUR RATING SYSTEM

Before we discuss the subjects under which the employee is to be evaluated, let us examine the different mechanics of rating. We wish, let us say, to have on paper an indication of whether or not one of our people is doing a certain part of his job. The simplest way would be to draw a line down the middle of a sheet of paper and put "Yes" on one side and "No" on the other, and we would be in the appraisal business. This would be a trifle primitive, to be sure, and we would want more than that. In most cases we want to know not only whether he is doing the job, but how well he is doing it.

Perhaps we could use three columns instead of two: Good, Average, and Bad. This is more sophisticated, but it has a weakness in practice. One of the many reasons that managers dislike appraisals is that they fear to affect the destiny of their people. This is ridiculous, of course; you must affect the destiny of your staff in some way or another. This reluctance to praise or damn anyone makes the "Average" column most attractive to the appraisor, and he tends to mark his workers as Average-average-average, which doesn't get us anywhere very fast.

There are other methods. One of the most common is using the scale of numbers from 1 through 10, in which 10 is perfect, 1 is horrible, and 9 through 2 covers the range in between. You put a ring around whichever number seems to describe the situation best. Even here there is a cowardly tendency to mark the man as 5 or 6. I recall getting over this problem in one company in a rather naughty way, although it did work. We used the 1 to 10 scale, but ours looked like this:

$$10 \quad 9 \quad 8 \quad 7 \qquad 4 \quad 3 \quad 2 \quad 1$$

Without the six and five, managers were forced to come down on one side of the fence or the other.

Some think marking a human being by numbers is cold and unfeeling, and for those there are other ways. This type of thing is quite popular:

a   Excellent
b   Consistently above average
c   Average
d   Consistently below average
e   Poor

This may seem to provide only five distinctions, but we can link this method to a block pattern, and instead of five distinctions or ratings you have an infinite number. Suppose you have decided to mark

your man in the "b" or "Consistently above average" block. You can
mark him thus:

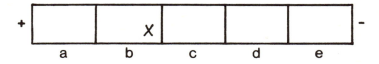

This would mean that while he is indeed above average, the
distinction is a fine one. Or, you could mark him near the left side of
the box, which would indicate that he is as close as he can get to the
"a" block, and only his irritating habit of telling dirty jokes in the
typists' pool is keeping him from being an "a."

THE BEER SYSTEM

There is another method of rating which I almost hesitate to
unleash because I am still kicking it around. Occasionally late at
night when my old buddy Johnnie Walker and I are sitting around
and straightening out all the management problems of the world, I
have the feeling that this is the appraisal rating system to end all
systems. Next morning I'm not sure. You like it, use it. You don't
like it, Mr. Walker and I will work on it some more.

It is based on the concept that while it is important to know where
the appraisee is now, it is far more important to know where he is
going. You would certainly like to know whether your man is, say, a
7 or a 3 on the 1 to 10 scale. But isn't it more to the point to know
whether he is improving or deteriorating? Surely, because this tells
you whether you are doing a decent job of managing him!

If my system has nothing else, at least it is the most simple one
you ever saw. It is merely two blocks, with a plus sign on the left and
a minus sign on the right. It works like this: you have a man on your
team, and his performance at the moment in the area you are
examining is not quite average. He has a long way to go before you
will be happy with him. You therefore put an X somewhat below the
halfway mark:

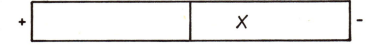

He's not doing too good, you say? But here is the whole point of this type of rating: he isn't all that good at the moment *but he is improving*. Under your careful guidance he is polishing off the rough spots, he recognizes his failings, he is doing something about them. And your rating tells you very clearly that this is so because next to that X you draw an arrow pointing left, towards the + mark, or "good" side of the bar.

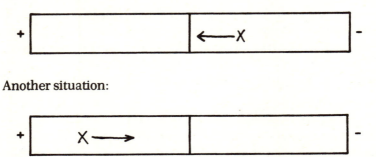

Another situation:

Do you need to be told what is happening here? A very unhappy situation, this. Your man is good, well above the halfway mark, but he is going sour. His performance in the area you are examining is falling off, and you had better take immediate action if you are to save him from the ranks of tomorrow's unemployed.

The point of this system is that it is dynamic. It shows movement, either for better or for worse. And that is a whole lot more useful than simply knowing where he is now. Another thing I like about it is that it is simple, and the simpler we can keep this, the better.

WHAT TO APPRAISE

So much for the mechanical side of rating. We need to look now at some of the areas in which we are to do the appraising. What exactly do we want to know about our man? Well, this depends on the job he is doing. Clearly, the appraisal of a statistical clerk covers very different ground from that of a workshop foreman or a salesman, and the forms would have to be different.

The points listed below would cover the job responsibilities of a typical salesman, but even here, a distinction must be made among different types of salesmen. I have chosen a sales job in the fast-moving consumer field as the example. This person sells detergents and allied products to supermarkets and chain stores. While many of the areas are common to all selling, there are specific sections (such as Merchandising) which have nothing to do with, for instance, an industrial salesman. The four main sections of performance, procedures, personality and potential cover, respectively, how well he is doing his job, *how* he goes about doing it, his mental approach to the job, and where he can go in the company.

APPRAISAL FORM (SALESMAN, CONSUMER DIVISION)

Performance

SALES VOLUME

Consistency of target attainment

New business attained

Old business recovered

SALES QUALITY

Selling across the range

Merchandising

Trading up

Area coverage

Credit control

Procedures

SELF-ORGANIZATION

Time and territory planning

Appointments

Economy of operation

Literature, samples, demonstration kits

PAPERWORK

Call planning

Call reports

Expense accounts

KNOWLEDGE

Products

Competitive products

Competitive activity

Customers

Industry

Territory

Personality

ATTITUDE

Towards company and management

Towards the job

Product confidence

MOTIVATION

Initiative

Personal goals

Persistence

MATURITY

Self-confidence

Reliability

Adaptability to circumstances

Dependability under pressure

COOPERATION

With superior

With internal staff

Conformity to company policy

Potential   (Note: It is probably not advisable to discuss this section with appraisee.)

IN PRESENT POSITION

ELSEWHERE IN THE COMPANY

Remarks

WEAKNESSES

Degree (mild or serious)

What action can be taken

What objectives can be set

STRENGTHS

To be recognized and discussed

APTITUDES AND LEANINGS

Is he specially suited to any particular type of work, either as an extension of his present job or in a different sphere of the company's activities?

CHANGE SINCE PREVIOUS APPRAISAL

Significant general improvement

Improvement in some respects

No significant change

Deterioration in some respects
General deterioration

(Note: Markings for each section must not be averaged. Each is to be considered separately.)

As we can see, appraisal forms for internal office people and production or technical staff will have different subsections. However, the four P's comprising the main sections (Performance, Procedures, Personality, and Potential) will probably be the same. Under Performance there would be a subsection covering accuracy and another for neatness in a typical typists' appraisal, just as there would be a subsection on care of machinery in the form for a toolmaker.

A GOOD POLICY

All very well, but selecting the areas of appraisal is not much of a problem. It is setting oneself up as a criticizer of others which bugs most managers. How can it seem to be anything but a witch hunt to the appraisee? Surely he is going to see it as an excuse for not giving him the raise he is expecting, or as the first step in firing him?

It doesn't have to be that way at all. I have a client company where, far from the staff resenting or fearing the appraisal, it is common for a man to say to his manager, "Hey, isn't it about time that you did another appraisal on me?" How have they managed to instill this excellent attitude towards appraisals in their people? Quite simple. They have made three things crystal clear regarding their appraisal system:

1. Appraisals are not done only at the level of the workforce. *Every* level is appraised, from janitor to director. This disposes of the "witch hunt for the proletariat" idea.
2. The mere fact that you are being appraised is a good indication that management thinks you are worth the time and effort. They don't bother to pick specks out of rotten apples.
3. It is continually emphasized that if the appraisee is not happy with his appraisal, if he believes that it is not a true

reflection of his performance, or that the appraisor is biased against him, he can walk the appraisal and the appraisor into the office of the next man up. There is a true open-door policy on appraisals, right up to the highest level, and the company is not fooling on this one. They really mean it.

Not difficult, is it?

THE NEED FOR DISCUSSION

I have had managers tell me that they have an active appraisal system, but, of course, the appraisal is not discussed with the appraisee. A man's rating, I am told smugly, is "highly confidential." Well, of course it is confidential. But if it is so confidential that you can't discuss it with the man himself, then forget the whole thing, don't waste your time. *The entire concept of appraisals is that they are discussed freely, fully, and frankly with the man himself.* If proof of this is needed, here it is:

I am a salesman and you are my manager. I am in my car, driving between calls, and I am thinking, "My future is good in this outfit. My sales volume is climbing, I brought in two new accounts last week, I came top in the product knowledge quiz at the last sales meeting, and my customer relations is excellent. I should be due for promotion, or at least a good raise, any time now."

At the very moment that I am saying this to myself, you are sitting in your office, thinking, "Michael has no future in this outfit. His territory coverage is terrible, he nevers sends in his call reports on time, he antagonizes the order clerks, he hasn't the faintest idea of credit control, and he dresses like a gutter bum. Unless he improves he is going to get fired any time now."

Is it possible that you and I are thinking about the same person? Why do I *honestly* feel that my future is bright while you *honestly* feel that I have no future? Why are our ideas poles apart? Because you and I have never sat down, belly to belly, and talked about my job. I don't even know that the failings you are grumbling about are so important. You don't even know how proud I am of my achievements, and how determined I am that I reach the top spot on the sales graph. How could we know? ESP?

There is no substitute for the manager and the salesman closing the door, loosening their collars, rolling up their sleeves, and talking about the job, and there never will be. The appraisal form's importance is simply that it provides a set of parameters, a starting point, a common ground for the talk.

Well then, why not show him how you have marked him on Potential? Well, suppose you are marking him high under this section, and have been for the last few appraisals. He is likely to go home and tell his wife that any minute now he is scheduled for a nice fat promotion. But there may simply be no slot for him to slide up into at this time. This can lead to frustration on his part and the feeling that performance isn't rewarded in this company, and you may lose a good man who, with a little patience, could one day fill your chair as you move up.

Of course, whether you choose to discuss the subject of potential depends on the man himself. It may well be that he is mature enough to recognize that his future is bright in the company if he bides his time and keeps slogging away; the wait will be worth his while. At least the fact that his appraisal interview with you acknowledges that his worth is being recognized by his superior is a tremendous comfort and assurance to him.

This last point by itself is sufficient reason for the appraisal system. Men will work very hard at jobs which are, because of circumstances prevailing at the time, perhaps below their capacity and potential *as long as they know that management is aware of that potential.* People leave companies in scores because "The boss didn't realize what a hell of a job I was doing."

When we appraise a man without discussing our appraisal, the whole value of the exercise is lost. Indeed, it is often the practice to give the man a blank copy of the form the day before the interview, ask him to fill it in on himself as you are going to do, and the next day to sit down with the two completed forms and use them as a basis for the discussion. If you do this you will be astonished, perhaps, to find that he often marks himself lower on certain sections that you have! This is great. It means that he has already conceded the need for improvement and is looking to you to help him with that improvement.

I cannot overemphasize the importance of utilizing the appraisal not so much to look at past performance, which, after all, is history, but to set up guidelines and objectives for *future* performance. Certainly we look at what has happened in his past, but only to assess needs and deficiencies which will be corrected starting right now.

CONDUCTING THE INTERVIEW

The success or failure of the appraisal system depends entirely on the interview itself, and the success of failure of the interview depends entirely on the attitude of the manager who conducts it. Let me give you from memory excerpts from two interviews to illustrate this. The first happened shortly after an appraisal system had been installed in a company in which I was working. I was in the branch office, and the branch manager was grumbling about this new system which had been foisted on him by head office. I did my best to convince him that the idea was sound and valuable, without much success, and he prevailed on me to sit in on the first of the interviews with his staff. This I was reluctant to do. I pointed out that the interview should be private, but I let myself be persuaded because I had grave doubts about the manager's ability and attitude and I wanted to discover the worst. The scenario went something like this:

Salesman: What's all this about, chief?

Manager: It's another piece of [expletive deleted] from head office. Come on, let's get it over with. I want you back on the road. [*Examines the form*] I'm marking you 3 out of 10 for Product Knowledge. You're weak on that.

Salesman: That's not fair! I deserve more than that!

Manager: The hell you do! Last week you didn't even know what the jiggle factor was on our model 70.

Salesman: Well, okay. But 3 out of 10!

Manager: All right, all right, stop crying. Make it 5. What the hell, nobody's going to read it anyhow. [*Beer is holding his head and reminding himself that grown men don't weep in public*]

Salesman [*Plaintively*]: If nobody's going to read it, what are we doing it for?

That was not exaggerated—it happened. In example number two, I sat in while a manager explained the appraisal system to his team before starting the individual interviews:

Some of you have indicated that you are worried about the new appraisal system, and I would like to make clear that there is nothing to worry about. The only reason for the system is that it helps me to do a better job for you. I am a manager, which simply means a man who directs the activities of a group of people. Now, my boss judges me on how well my group, meaning you men, operates. Therefore it is my job to help you to operate as effectively as possible, and the form which you have in front of you is simply an aid in achieving this. But get one thing clear. In the discussions we are going to have there will be no complaints from me about substandard performance. This is not a bind and grind session. Suppose that I mark one of you "below average" for Prospecting. Okay, that's my assessment of what happened in the past, but there is no black mark on you for that. It means only one thing—that you and I are going to work on that aspect of your job for the next six months so that the next time we do one of these forms, I am going to be forced to mark you "above average." How does that sound to you?

The basic difference between the two managers? Attitude, only attitude. The one's attitude was that he considered the scheme a complete waste of time, and he did a great job of transmitting this same attitude to his staff member. The other manager started right because his own attitude towards the scheme was right, and he got this across to his men before he had a single interview.

Here are a few points to help make the appraisal interview run sweetly:

1. Preferably in a meeting of the whole group, explain the appraisal program fully and clearly. Expect questions and be prepared to answer them. If a meeting is not feasible, then the letter of explanation should be a masterpiece of communication.
2. Give each man his appraisal form at least one full day ahead of the interview, and show him exactly how to fill it in.
3. Set a date and time for the interview, and do your very best not to let anything cancel it.

4. Be ready for the interview—desk clear, telephone quiet, office private. *Nobody,* not even the company president, comes in. (Come to think of it, *especially* not the president.)

5. Put him at his ease—cigarettes, coffee, chit chat.

6. Briefly review the reasons for the appraisal and what you hope to accomplish.

7. Go through each section, asking for his assessment and giving him yours. Allow plenty of time for this.

8. Explain your rating, *but on no account be drawn into an argument on it.* You justify it, you do not defend it.

9. Never complain, threaten, grumble, or sound off in any way in this interview. If you have to do any of these, then do it at some other time. Keep your cool.

10. Be quick to recognize any improvement and all good points, no matter how small.

11. Using the ratings, set objectives for the future, *and get his commitment on them.*

12. Thank him for his cooperation, and remind him that this will be a regular thing from now on.

SOME OFT-ASKED QUESTIONS

It might be best to end this chapter by trying to answer some of your questions. What follows are typical questions which are put to me in management clinics on appraisal.

How often should appraisals be done? There is no set time, but most companies seem to run them every six months, and this seems reasonable. I know one company which has their regular appraisal once a year, but if they need to make a decision of any sort about one of their people—promote, transfer, train, or fire him—they will do a snap appraisal. I'm not sure that I like this very much. People quickly realize that the snap appraisal means something different, and their attitude can suffer because of it.

Is there any point in the worker doing an appraisal of his boss? I have been asked this question dozens of times and the answer is still the same: No. Forget it; it won't do one single thing for anyone. If all appraisals should be open, that is, if the boss should see the appraisal of him by his subordinate, then it won't be the truth. It will either be better than the truth or worse, and neither is going to help.

Should an appraisal be done just before the time for salary increases? No. The appraisal gets tied too closely to the money angle in the man's mind, and he becomes too concerned about his raise to get much good from the appraisal interview. Also, it sounds as though the appraisal is an excuse for cutting his increase, which is a certain way of destroying any good results from it.

Is there any time when an exception could be made to the one-to-one interview? Should a senior man ever sit in? I can't see it. Willing cooperation and complete frankness is difficult enough to achieve with only two of you. Obviously, you are going to discuss your staff appraisals with your immediate superior after the interviews, but I don't see that he has any business playing gooseberry in the interview itself.

Why should a good manager need a formal appraisal system? Isn't it his job to be continually evaluating his people on an informal bases? Certainly it is his job to evaluate performance, and he does it every day, not only twice a year. He has informal chats with his people over a couple of beers and often these can be very rewarding, but they are not a substitute for formal appraisal. Only by using the form, by making the interview formal, by setting aside definite times for it, by patiently going through every facet of the job, can he really help his subordinate correct his weaknesses and build on his strengths.

The happy thought to take away from this chapter could be this: *Your people have a right to know what you think of their work.* Just as you have a right to know what your superior thinks of your performance, so your subordinates have a right to know how you rate them. They have a right to discuss on-the-job problems and their solutions. The appraisal system is the best, if not the only, way to do this effectively.

13

The Scientific Art of Organizing Salesmen

A "scientific art" may seem like a contradiction in terms, but organization of things is a science, and organization of people is an art, and here we are concerned with both—the organization of a salesman and his territory.

While organization in a sales office can, regrettably, become a very complicated process, let us never forget that the real reason for it is very simple. Everything we do is aimed at getting the salesman to make the optimum number of effective calls on the right people in as economical a way as possible. This is oversimplifying a little, but simplifying is a good fault (most sales organization is far too complicated). Notice that we say *optimum* number of calls, not *maximum* number. Notice that these calls must be on the right people. Notice that they must be made economically.

By making the optimum number of calls we mean using the correct call frequency. Someone selling microfilm installations might be correct in calling only twice a year on a prospective customer, while someone selling frozen foods might have to call twice a week on a large supermarket. When we say "calling on the right people," we don't mean whether to see Mr. Finkle or Mr. Fussbinder at the Hardsell Trading Company. We mean the ratio of service calls on present customers to cold calls on prospective customers, of calls on distributors compared to calls on end-users, of calls in the city compared to calls in rural areas, that sort of things. Finally, when we stress the need for economy, we are thinking of the salesman who brings in good sales figures but does it by chalking up far too much mileage, piling up unnecessary expenses. Doing things economically is part of organization, too.

CREATING YOUR TERRITORIES

Let us assume that as a sales manager, your district stretches from here right across to there. You have a force of seven salesmen, each with his own territory within your overall district. You may decide that the first thing to do in organizing your district is to examine the individual territories and, if necessary, to reapportion them for greater efficiency. Great idea. How are you going to go about it? Well, you have seven salesmen, so the obvious way is to divide the district into seven territories, taking into account the number and importance of customers, the square mileage to be covered, the balance of town and country in each, and generally looking for a fair distribution of sales figures. Then you assign each salesman to a territory and you are in business, right?

Wrong.

This is the way it is always done, and it is always the wrong way. We split the area by the number of salesmen we happen to have in our team, when the logical way would surely be to decide how many salesmen we need to give us optimum territory coverage. Why seven salesmen, merely because we happen to have inherited seven from the previous manager? Why not five, or nine?

The ideal way is to wipe all territorial boundaries off the map and start from scratch, but a less drastic way is to look at each territory and decide exactly how big it should be. Doing this might show us that we can cut the number of territories (and therefore salesmen) down to five, or that we should increase it to nine. There is a way to do this, and it always astonishes me that it isn't used more often, because it is simple in concept and easy in practice. Here it is:

1. Rate all customers in the territory. The rating can be by potential sales volume, in descending order of importance (say, A. B, C, D, and E), or you may prefer to grade by type of customer (distributor, wholesaler, retailer), depending on which suits your business. In a typical territory you could have 10 A's, 75 B's, 120 C's, 40 D's, and 15 E's.

2. *Determine optimum call frequency*. You might decide that A's should be called on 25 times a year or twice a month, down to where the E's will get three calls a year if they're lucky.

3. *Count number of calls necessary per year*. This is simple arithmetic based on your figures from (1) and (2). Ten A customers to be called on 25 times a year is 250 calls for the A's. Do the same for the other ratings and add up the results to get the grand total of calls necessary to service that territory for a full year.

4. *Decide on a realistic call rate*. And don't be tempted to apply the old clichés about call rates, such as industrial salesmen, eight calls a day; consumer products, fifteen a day, and so on. Consider physical area, type of customer, range of products, and all the other variables before you decide on a realistic number of calls per day. This is an important step, so get it right. The very best way to get an accurate figure is the obvious one: get out into the territory and work it yourself for a few days.

5. *Calculate the number of calls possible for one salesman in a year*. Most salesmen have between 180 and 200 selling days in a year. It doesn't sound like very much, but when you take into consideration weekends, holidays, sick leave, sales meetings, and so forth, it works out about right. Multiply the number of selling days by the daily call rate from (4) and you have the number of calls possible in that territory for a year.

6. *Divide (5) into (3)*. And, probably, get the shock of your life. This is the only scientific way to determine how big a territory should be and, by extension, how many salesmen you need to cover your whole area.

There are variables, naturally. It may be that an A customer does not need to be called on at the A rate for some good reason, and he can be downgraded to B or C. It may be that you and your salesman decide that a certain E customer, if he is called on often enough, could turn into a B, and you would decide to rate him as a B for call frequency. Also, remember that we have been looking at present customers only, but what about prospecting? Time must be allowed for this, and while a toothpaste salesman will do very little prospecting if any (one call in thirty, say), a typewriter salesman may spend most of his selling day cold-calling on prospects.

Such variables can be built into the sum without destroying the overall concept, and until you have done this sum for every individual territory in your district you have no idea of whether you are under- or overstaffed, whether you are asking the impossible of your salesmen, or whether you are running a home for tired salesmen where they are doing a half day's work for a full day's salary.

Once you have done this you have mastered the basic organization for your area, and apart from keeping a close watch on circumstances to see if you need to do it again (for instance if a major industrial plant or a large shopping complex is built in one of the territories), there is little to do which your salesmen themselves cannot do.

CUTTING DOWN ON PAPERWORK

We have to examine the extremely boring business or paperwork, and we may as well get to it now. No doubt in your company there are many different pieces of paper which your salesmen have to shuffle around—claim reports, action reports, lost sale reports, customer complaint forms, returned stock forms, and so on. Most salesmen complain bitterly that the company is turning them into clerks and pen-pushers, that they have far too much paperwork. Sometimes they are right, sometimes wrong. Salesmen tend to scream in agony as a pure reflex action whenever a new form is produced.

If you are getting static from your salesforce about paperwork, you might like to try something which has worked for me in the past. Clear your desk of everything on it, and on the empty surface put one copy of every single form, report, account, and memo which your salesmen have to read, process, fill in, or check. Spread them all out, giving them plenty of space. Then pick each piece up one at a time and examine it carefully with these questions in mind:

Why was this produced in the first place?
Is that reason still valid, or has it fallen away?

Does it help the salesman, directly or indirectly, to do a better job?
If it is still really necessary, can't it be made more simple?
Can it be incorporated into another form, making one out of two?

This little exercise, if it is done completely objectively and with an open mind, could cut down on the weight of paperwork with which your men are burdened, and in the process it could make your own job less paper oriented. Try it.

THE CRUCIAL CALL PLAN

Let's concentrate on the two pieces of paper which *every* salesmen *must* be using regularly. They are the call plan and the call report. No matter what a salesman sells, how he sells it, or who he sells it to, these two are essential. Why? Simply because if he is not using them, then he is working too hard and not getting the results he should from that work.

Take call planning first. This form says: "This is what I intend to do." Although it is neater if you have an official company form for this. Any salesman can turn a piece of paper on its side and draw a horizontal line across it, with morning above the line, afternoon below it. He can draw two lines if he works morning, afternoon, and evening. Four vertical lines give him five spaces for Monday, Tuesday, Wednesday, Thursday, and Friday, and he is in busines. Many companies use a form which covers an entire call cycle of five or six weeks. Salesmen in such industries as fast-moving consumer items, ethical drugs, and farm supplies use them as a way of life.

Why is call planning essential? Because without it a salesman wakes up every morning out of a job. He has to go and find work to do, every day of his life. That's working too hard, and who needs it when planning is so simple? Without a planning sheet your salesmen travel too far each month, backtracking and recovering territory already covered. They miss calls; they have too much to do today and not enough to do tomorrow. They are trying to cross the ocean without a map, rudder, or compass.

In almost every sales clinic I run, at least one salesman says, "Planning is all right for some people, but my sort of selling doesn't allow for planning. I can plan a day or a week perfectly, and halfway through it I hit an emergency and have to drop everything and handle it, and my plan goes down the drain." Two comments on that. First, what makes this man think that he is so different? Emergencies happen to all of us and they often wreck the best-laid plans. Second, if this happens we need a plan more than ever, because a plan not only tells us, "This is what you intend to do," it also tells us, "This is what you meant to do but didn't." And that information is just as important.

The best news I can give to any salesman who has never used call planning is simply this: If you have a piece of paper telling you what to do when you wake up on Monday morning, it is a hell of a lot easier to get out of bed. You have somewhere to go; you have a *job*.

THE INVALUABLE CALL REPORT

Next, call reporting. A call report says: "This is what I have achieved." We might start by giving a salesman's definition of a call report: It is a piece of paper dreamed up by some clown in head office to keep himself in a job, and it is a complete waste of time for a working salesman. Most salesmen would go along with this definition, and it can be true. Call reports can be a big yawn, a routine thing which hits the manager's desk like junk mail. If you feel this way, then you are ignoring a vital link between the field and the office. You are rejecting the best source of information on which to plan sales strategy, and you are reinforcing the salesman's already low opinion of paperwork.

Most call report forms are badly designed, being long on routine information and short on special information. But it is this special information which makes the report worth while. By special information we mean such things as any significant change in the customer's buying habits, competitive activity (new products, special discounts, advertising campaigns), any indication of change in customer's financial situation, movement in customer's staff (promotions, transfers, a new contact man), change in customer's attitude towards us, success stories about our product's performance, that sort of thing.

But what about the salesman who sell cigars to corner shops and makes up to forty calls a day. Do we really expect him to find time to write all that stuff down? Yes and no. That salesman's daily report will be very brief, probably not more than a series of check marks on a list of customers—*until he has special information on a customer which merits recording.* When he does have some special information, he writes it down, but his day is such a rush that he does not spend much time on it. A quick note in his diary gives him the reminder to include it in his report when he sits down at the end of the day to write it. This customer has been given a new display rack by the competition, that one had two delayed deliveries this month, the other one is now buying five cases at a time to get the bigger discount, and he has agreed to a display window. Vital information, all this, and if there is space for it on the form, it is easy to put down.

I firmly believe that the salesman's attitude towards reports comes from the manager's attitude. One salesman in a training clinic listened to my plea for good reporting from the field and muttered during the coffee break, "Don't sell me on writing reports. Sell my manager on reading them when I write them." How many times have I said that we can't fool the people who work for us? A manager who insists on the submission of regular reports and then doesn't read them (and therefore cannot act on them) is creating a most unhappy attitude in his men.

The value of the call report is manifold. First, it is up-to-date, "hard news" information from the front line, written by the only man who really knows what is going on there—the salesman in his own territory. Second, it contains information of long-term value which can be transferred to the customer's record card. Third, it has information of inestimable value for use at the end of the year, both by the salesman and his manager.

I have urged salesmen who voice the complaint that management does not read their reports to carry on and fill them in meticulously, even if they know that their manager makes paper hats out of them. They should do this not for the original which is sent in to the office *but for the copy which the salesman keeps for himself.* From these copies the pro salesman can, at the end of the year, find out where the money is coming from (which type of customer is most profitable). He can determine, based on present sales and future potential, just how much time to spend in what parts of his territory. He can discover his own strengths and weaknesses in prospecting, call backs, trading up, expanding the product range in old customers, selling related items, etc.

A gold mine—that is what a good reporting system is. It's a veritable gold mine of information, and if the salesman is not using it properly, then he is working too hard.

You can change your salesmen's attitude towards reporting, not by threatening him with all sorts or punishment if he does not send reports in regularly, but by showing him that you consider reports to be important documents. You can do this by discussing with him points of interest from recent reports, by asking him to expand on some particular report, and best of all, by taking action on a recommendation from his reports and, if feasible, letting the rest of the team know that it was the salesman's idea and that it came from one of his reports.

That's it on Organization, and if it seems less than it should be, remember what we are trying to achieve. We want our salesmen to make the *optimum* number of *effective* calls on the *right* people, *economically*. The concept is simple. Let's keep it that way.

14

The Rewarding Art of Delegation

I was once invited to a farewell party for an executive being transferred overseas on promotion. He stood up and made the usual sort of speech and I listened with half an ear until he said something which prodded me into wakefulness. He was talking about management practice, and what woke me up was one sentence. He said, "One of the biggest problems of the middle manager today is that he spends so much time doing the *urgent* things that he has no time to do the *important* things."

I don't know whether than man was quoting or whether he worked that out himself, but ever since I heard it over ten years ago, it has changed my way of thinking, and it seems a good way to set the tone of this chapter. I don't know if he meant to or not, but that speaker was discussing the art of *delegation*.

The dictionary defines delegation as "the entrusting of authority to a deputy." But that is only half the story. The *business* definition would have to go further and introduce another word: "the entrusting of authority *and responsibility* to a deputy." You must have both together, of course. If you give a man responsibility without authority you will drive him out of his mind with frustration. Whereas if you give him authority without responsibility—well, I have been looking for a job like that all my life. The two must be very closely matched, the one with the other.

EXCUSES FOR NOT DELEGATING

Most managers pay lip service to delegation, because delegation is a hard thing to knock. But they often resist doing it—and when they are forced into it they go about it in the wrong way. If you are in the vast majority of managers, then you do not delegate as you should. Why not? Here are some excuses for not delegating. Pick the one which most appeals to you:

I can do it better.
I can do it faster.
It would take so much time to show someone else how to do it that I might as well do it myself.
I have always done it.
This one has got to be done right. I can't trust anyone else to do it.
It's my neck if Bartley fouls it up, not his.
If I start giving Bartley more important work to do, he will get ideas about a salary raise.
I happen to have the time to do it myself right now.
If I give it to Bartley he will think I'm getting lazy and am passing the dirty work to him.
He will come back with so many questions that I won't really be saving time at all.
My own boss will think I'm not doing a proper job if I pass my work on to others.

Does any one of those fit you? Well, they are excuses, not reasons, and you ought to be ashamed of yourself.

TWO REASONS TO DELEGATE

Why delegation? There are two entirely separate reasons to delegate, and they have nothing whatever to do with each other. Either one by itself would be ample reason for delegation, and when we take them together we realize that delegation is not an interesting and possibly valuable management skill, but is one of the most vitally important things a manager does.

The first reason for a sound delegation program is simply that *people need to grow.* Most people have an urgent and fundamental need to become bigger and more valuable to themselves and to the companies they work for, and this can be done only by delegating authority and responsibility to them as they are capable of absorbing and using it.

The second reason is just as simple and just as true: *Higher income people should do higher return work.* If you, as a relatively higher income man, are doing work which, directly or indirectly, is bringing in a lower return, then you are cheating your company. It doesn't matter if you get to work at dawn, hurl yourself at your desk and work until midnight—you are cheating your company.

I once set in on a meeting to decide which manager to promote to a higher position. A fairly obvious choice was a man who had the experience, the stature, and the attitude to do the bigger job adequately. He was finally passed over because one of the senior executives said, "No. If we pull him out of his present job there is nobody to replace him, and it's no good filling one slot by emptying another one."

A real tragedy, this. The man could have done the new job, but he didn't get it because he didn't *deserve* it. He had made no provision in his team for a man to replace him. He had fallen down on a vital part of his job. He had cheated the company.

An uncle of mine was, I suppose, a classic success story, since he had risen from an accounting clerk to become the head of a large group of companies. I had always admired him, and one day I asked him the secret of his success. "Michael," he said, "I do have a secret if you would like to hear it. I have followed it all my life."

Suddenly I was all ears. I was about to learn the secret of success in business by a man who claimed that secret had taken him right to the top! He said, "This is what you do: Learn the job of the man above you—teach your job to the man below you." And exactly eight of those sixteen words means *delegation*.

RULES FOR SUCCESSFUL DELEGATING

You may believe that since you have a team of only five salesmen, this big idea of delegation has nothing to do with you. Heck, how could you start a delegation program in a group that size, and, anyway, why should you?

Well, you can and you should. Don't be put off by the thought that a delegation program is too complex for your present circumstances. We are talking about something very simple in concept. Sit back at this moment and ask yourself this: if you were promoted tomorrow, which of your men could move into your job immediately? Dirty question, huh? There isn't really one of them who could do it, is there?

Well, that is what we are doing this exercise for. If you can't produce a man who could take over from you immediately, who is the *likeliest* man? Why? Let us be careful that we are not making any emotional decisions here. Pull out the last few appraisals you did on your people and decide that way rather than making a snap decision based on yesterday's performance.

Very well then, you have picked Rutherford as the most likely candidate and you are ready to build him into a potential successor to you. A few points follow:

1. *Find out if he wants it.* Do you remember that fascinating character citizen A in the chapter on motivation? If Rutherford is a citizen A then he most likely will not want the extra responsibility, and you will have chosen the wrong man. It won't be easy to get the truth from him about this because we have so ordered our society that we have made it clear to everyone that anyone who is not ambitious to rise to the top is shamelessly anti social, is undermining the very structure of modern socio-economic philosophy, and is also a reprobate. Unless you have already communicated fairly deeply with Rutherford, he will probably say that yes, he likes the idea, while secretly he is appalled by it. Convince him that there is no black mark against him if he does not want it, and that he will still be a valued member of the team.

2. *Tell him what you intend to do.* Unless you do this he will go home and tell his wife that the boss is off his head and that he is piling all the work on to his subordinates' shoulders. He must see that what he is doing now is part of an overall plan. Incidentally, need we emphasize that merely transferring a large, conical heap of paper from your desk to Rutherford's is not delegation? We are talking about a planned program of educating Rutherford into a higher level of responsibility, not simply passing across to him any work which you don't like doing.

3. *Slow and easy does it.* You have taken long enough to get into delegation at all, so there is certainly no hurry now. One new thing at a time is the recipe here, and make sure that he has absorbed the information and acquired the skill to do that one job before you hit him with the next.

4. *Let him learn by doing it himself.* You can show, you can tell, you can explain, and you can demonstrate, but you learned to ride a bicycle by *riding* a bicycle—there is no other way. Finally, after all the teaching, he has to do it himself. He will fall off the bicycle; he will get discouraged and wonder if he will ever be able to do it; but eventually he will learn, and the only way he will learn is by doing it himself.

5. *Supervise closely at first.* Here you have to tread the fine line between breathing down his neck and throwing him in the deep end and walking away. You must show him that you are there, that your door is truly open if he has to cry for help, but you don't want him to feel that your hand is ready to snatch the job away from him the first time he looks like he will make a mistake.

Accept the fact that he will make mistakes: it is the first sign of learning. When he does, and comes to you with a long face expecting to be reprimanded, surprise him. Show him that you recognize that the mistake came about through lack of experience, not through stupidity. He didn't do it properly because you didn't teach him properly, so show him again and strengthen his spirit. You can break his spirit very easily at this time by saying, "All right, give it back to me. Maybe you're not ready for it yet."

The first thing to do if you fall off a horse is to get back on again immediately. In the same way, when Rutherford comes to you with something he has done wrong, the wisest thing to do is to show him how to avoid the error and give him something else to do immediately. This will have the effect of taking his mind off his failure and on to the best way to make the new task a success. It will do even more than that: it will show him that you have not lost faith in him.

6. *Let him do it his way.* Easy to say, very hard to do. Say you are a surgeon watching a young doctor performing an operation you have taught him. You can have one of three thoughts in your mind as you watch him at work. (1) "He is doing the operation exactly as I taught him to. The way is valid, and the result will be satisfactory." No problem. (2) "He is not doing it as I taught him, and this is not a valid way of doing it; the result will be unsatisfactory." Again, no problem. You stop him and show him the right way. (3) "He is not

performing the operation as I taught him to, *but his way is sound, and the result will be satisfactory.*" It is in this third situation that you show how good you are as a delegator. Are you going to stop him and say, "No, that is not the way I taught you; do it my way"? Or do you have the forebearance to grit your teeth and let him do it his way, as long as it conforms with sound policies and procedures?

In fact, we can take the medical analogy a step further and ask ourselves whether we should not perhaps let him carry on, even if he does not conform to recognized practice. Maybe recognized practice is wrong. Ignaz Semmelweis, the Hungarian pioneer in obstetrics and antisepsis, threw away established procedure in maternity homes and saved the lives of thousands of women. Perhaps Rutherford has hit on a way of doing something which would revolutionize the art of management! All right, it isn't very likely. But the point remains—let us not slap him down if he departs from recognized practice simply because we are not used to doing it that way.

7. Counsel often. When he realizes that you really mean this business of delegation, he will feel a mixture of pride and fright— pride that you have picked him out of the bunch and fright at the responsibility. Now is the time to build him up, encourage him, and give him confidence through fairly frequent gab sessions. These should generally be on the informal side, perhaps outside the office over a snort or two. You can build a very close working relationship with Rutherford in this way, and when you do it successfully you are doing two very important things. You are grooming him to take over from you eventually, and you are freeing yourself from the more routine work in order to concentrate on more important, higher-income work.

That will do as the basis for a simple delegation program, and there is nothing there which is too difficult or dangerous for any manager.

Many managers fall into the error of believing that when they have set up a program such as this they themselves will be doing less work than before, and nothing could be further from the truth. You could end up with more work than you did before, but now it will be important work rather than merely urgent work. *Rutherford is doing the urgent work.*

WHAT TO DELEGATE

So far we have discussed only *how* to delegate and have said little about *what* to delegate. Although we can touch on it briefly, I can't help you much with this problem. Only you can decide what can be delegated because only you know your job. Luckily, there is a simple way to go about this, but only you can do it. Here's how:

Buy yourself a pocket notebook. You almost certainly have one already, but buy another one. Don't go for one with an alligator-skin cover, because after a month you are going to throw it away. Carry it with you everywhere you go for thirty days, and religiously write down everything you do which has the slightest relationship to your job, and how long you spend doing it. Don't cheat on this. No one will see it except you, so you might as well be honest. A typical day could have everything in it from dictating letters to calling on a special customer to checking expense accounts to attending a management meeting to telephoning the insurance company about your lost camera. Write it all down.

At the end of the month, get a lot of paper and categorize what kept you busy during the past month. Put down columns of your different types of activity, and the time you spent on each. This can be a mind-blowing experience, and the chances are that you will not want to show it to anyone else, especially your boss. When you have done that, ask yourself one question about each *type* of activity: "Why am I doing this?" Unless you can give yourself a satisfactory answer, ask yourself another question: "Could anyone else do it?" These two questions, carefully considered and answered, can put you on the road to a workable delegation program.

Whenever I think of the art of delegation, I remember an incident which has always seemed to illustrate the problems of this aspect of management. I once had an odd sort of job which was variously described as Chief Food Taster, the Torpedo Man, or simply 007. What it meant was that, among other things, I had to lean on people on behalf of the general manager. One day he called me in and told me that I was leaving for a trip to one of our branch offices. I didn't bother to ask when I was going because with this man it meant on the next available flight. I asked what the problem was.

"That's for you to find out," he said. "All I know is that Eddie has got things fouled up down there somehow. I write him a letter and it takes him a week to answer it. We ask for a stock count and it comes back a month late. Go down there and find out what the hell he is doing, and tell him that if he doesn't straighten out and fly right he will find himself in plenty of trouble!" That was the way he talked; Hard/Strong.

I made it to the flight in time, and we landed at about eight that evening. The branch office had been notified of my arrival and one of the salesmen was there to pick me up. "Where's Eddie?" I asked.

"Oh, he's at the office," the salesman said. "He's usually there about this time. Shall I take you there?"

"No way," I said. "Take me to my hotel. I'm going to sleep."

The next morning I sat down with Eddie and explained as tactfully as I could that unless he got his branch into a more current situation, then as far as he was concerned I represented a sort of Mafia kiss.

He threw up his hands. "What more can I do?" he asked in despair. "I'm here at daybreak every morning and I don't leave until late at night. I'm flat out all day long. What does the old man expect?"

At that moment his telephone rang. When he had finished the call he said, "Michael, I'm sorry, but we'll have to talk later. Another crisis. One of our biggest customers wants three cases of product right away and no arguments. Both trucks are already out, all the salesmen are in the field. I have to take it out myself."

I leaned forward. "Eddie," I said gently. "This is what we are talking about! Don't you understand that? You are not taking that order out of this building!"

"Great," he said. "Then we lose a big account. The boss is going to love that."

"I don't give a damn how you do it, but you are not the delivery boy around here," I said. We finally put a very surprised office janitor in a taxi with the three cases next to him and *he* became the temporary express delivery service of the company.

Higher-income people do higher-return work! Now of course this does not mean that as soon as a man assumes the title of manager he becomes too exalted to get his hands dirty. The good industrial sales manager keeps a pair of overalls and a hard hat in his car and they get used. The good consumer-products sales manager gets his feet trampled by children in supermarkets while he is fighting to set up a free-standing display. Managers won't keep the respect of their salesmen if they act as though they are allergic to the dust of a stockroom or the grease of a factory. But, *as a way of life,* higher-income people do higher-return work.

Delegate! Apart from the obvious advantages to your protégé, your team, and the company, it can be the most effective thing you do to ensure your own promotion.

15

Why Managers Fail

It is Friday evening, and I am drafting this on my way home from work. It's been one of those weeks. I'm sure you have experienced them—irritating, unsatisfying, nothing going quite right. By the time Friday comes around, you are wondering what on earth possessed you to get into your present line of work. And to top it off it is raining like hell, so if you intend to get your golf game in tomorrow you shall have to do it in an aqualung and flippers.

Hardly the ideal frame of mind for writing the final chapter of a book. On the other hand, since I have tried to be completely honest, not pretending that anything is easy when I know that it is very difficult indeed, my present attitude may be the best one for the job in hand, so let's get at it.

THE BAD NEWS

Why are there so many mediocre managers? Not really bad managers, but so many whose performance is barely adequate, is uninspired and uninspiring, and who simply don't seem to be able to produce a team of successful, profitable, and company-oriented salesmen? I have been involved with managers of salesmen for almost the whole of my business life, working under them, being one of them myself, and finally training them, and while I may not have the easy answer to what makes a good manager, I sure as hell know what makes a bad one. Let us take a look at the main reasons managers fail.

1. They vacillate between Hard and Soft management. A very serious fault, this, and fairly common among managers who, either because of inexperience or unsuitability for the job, are insecure. Certainly we need to be flexible in our management philosophy, but this is not flexibility. It is a desperate attempt to play the tune in different keys to different people, hoping that one will sound right. One day this man will thunder, "Do it or you will be in trouble!" If this doesn't work then on the next day he will beg, "Please do it, or I will be in trouble!" A manager who blows hot and cold like this loses all respect and engenders a cynical attitude in his men.

2. They have the salesman's point of view, not the company's. The manager was once a salesman himself, and the temptation is great to take the salesman's side against the company in any confrontation, no matter what the facts are. After all, the salesman is a person, easy to relate to and identify with, while the company is an impersonal, monolithic giant. There is also a sneaky feeling that standing up for the salesman is an easy way to get the whole team on your side, loyal and steadfast against dat ol' debbil, the company. This manager has apparently forgotten who put him in the job in the first place and who is paying him now.

3. They fail to represent the salesman. This seems to be a complete contradiction of the previous point, but there is a world of difference between taking the salesman's side *against* the company (which is inexcusable) and truly representing the sales team *to* the company when there are suggestions, ideas, problems, or genuine grievances to be transmitted to top management. This is a failure in upward communication, and it happens because the manager fears that his own position will be jeopardized. This is a very dangerous block in communication. People quickly resent it if they feel that their manager is afraid to act as their spokesman to the top. People leave the company and, as always, it is the good people who go.

4. They hide behind higher authority. This must be one of the most stupid faults of managers. Afraid to take responsibility for an instruction themselves, they will say, "This has got to be done—the big boss says so." This clearly implies, "I don't personally agree with this instruction, but it comes from on high and I suppose it has got to be done." Terrible! And the consequences are just as terrible: a sulky and rebellious team. What would you think of a man who, if he doesn't agree with an order from the top, won't fight it at the top?

5. *They fail to set standards.* No fair and just father would ever punish a child for drawing on the wall if he had not first made it clear that such a practice was unacceptable, yet many managers blame their people for not complying with policies and procedures when these have not been spelled out in the first place. Your man has a right to know what you expect of him, and his performance depends greatly on how well you set out the standards you expect him to follow.

6. *They try to please everybody.* Faced with conflict between two people, or two departments, they try to find a solution which will not offend either party. There is only one solution and that is the right one, and it often offends one side or the other. Very well, this is where human relations comes in. But human relations is not soft-pedalling in order to please everyone. What usually happens with the compromise solution is that we please nobody—and we still don't have the right solution.

7. *They fail to set an example.* Ah, at last. Now perhaps we have reached the real secret of why managers fail. They fail because (and this is the last time I shall say it) you cannot fool the people who work for you, and unless you practice what you preach, your preaching will be in vain. Some quotations from people more intelligent and articulate than I:

Samuel Johnson: *Example is always more efficacious than precept.*
Edmund Burke: *Example is the school of mankind, and they will learn at no other.*
Ralph Waldo Emerson: *There are only three ways to teach—by example, by example, by example.*

True. *Obviously* true. And yet we fail to see it. We talk the importance of planning and organization, and our people can see that we ourselves do not plan and are not organized. We stress that the company pays them for a full working day and they see us arriving late and leaving early. We hammer them for a poor company attitude and after three drinks on a Friday night, we start a diatribe against the company with the whole team as audience.

If there is one reason above all others for management failure then this is it. You are in the limelight, right there in the center of the stage, visible to your men at all times, and believe it, they are watching you. You must be above reproach. You stand on a higher level than theirs, and they expect you to conform to higher standards.

We all know that top management expects more of us than it does of the sales force, but what we often forget is that the sales force expects it too, and unless they see it, clearly and constantly, they lose faith in us, and they resent it when they find that the feet of their idol are solid clay.

That is the bad news.

THE GOOD NEWS

The good news, and you are surely intelligent enough to perceive it, is that all we need to do is turn this picture around. If managers fail because they *don't* set an example, is it true that managers succeed because they *do*?

Good heavens, yes! My job puts me in close and continual contact with managers. I know them. I know how they think and how they act; I know their triumphs and disasters, their weaknesses and their strengths. Among these managers are those who don't know any of the things we have covered in this book, who break all the golden rules of management, who are not, Lord help them, even very intelligent—and who yet run a successful, profitable, and company-oriented team. Why? Because they lead by example, by example, by example, and that is their secret.

I love to watch the way these managers inspire their men and set their hearts on fire. When I managed salesmen, I reached this pinnacle only very seldom, and I envy the manager who can do it as a way of life. I have a few of them as friends, and I value their friendship more than almost anything else.

I don't have the talent to put this final point on paper as well as I should like to, but never mind the singer, listen to the song: if you manage by example then you need little else to do your job.

I don't know if you have ever realized just how important your job is in a marketing organization. The old cliché is that in a selling company the most important job is that of the salesman, because nothing happens until somebody sells something. This may be true, but it is too facile. The real truth is that a salesman is only as good as the man directly in charge of him—and that's you.

I don't say that anything in this book will make your job easy, because managing salesmen can never be easy. I do say that if any of this helps you to avoid the bigger mistakes in management, and if you manage by example, you may just make it.

Good luck.

Index